I0532889

Empowering You!

12 Key Principles of Personal Growth

Anisa Marku

Copyright © 2024 by Anisa Marku

All rights reserved. No part of this publication may be reproduced, distributed, or transmitted in any form or by any means, including photocopying, recording, or other electronic or mechanical methods, without the prior written permission of the author, except in the case of brief quotations embodied in critical reviews and specific other non-commercial uses permitted by copyright law.

First Printing, 2024

Printed in the United States of America

DISCLAIMER

The information presented in this book is intended to provide general guidance and advice.

While every effort has been made to ensure the accuracy and completeness of the information, the author and publisher make no representations or warranties of any kind, express or implied, about the completeness, accuracy, reliability, suitability, or availability with respect to the content contained within this book.

The techniques, strategies, and examples provided in this book are based on the author's experience and research. However, individual results may vary, and the author and publisher disclaim any responsibility for any adverse effects or consequences resulting from the implementation of these techniques or strategies.

The content of this book is not intended to serve as a substitute for professional advice or guidance. Readers are encouraged to seek the advice of qualified professionals in relevant fields, such as career coaching, personal development, or goal-setting, before implementing any strategies discussed in this book.

The author and publisher shall not be liable for any loss or damage, including but not limited to direct, indirect, special, or consequential damages, arising from the use or reliance on information contained in this book or from any errors or omissions that may occur. The inclusion of any links or references to third-party websites, products, or services does not imply endorsement or guarantee of the accuracy, quality, or suitability of such content.

By reading this book, you acknowledge and agree to the above disclaimer. You understand that the author and publisher shall not be held responsible for any actions, decisions, or outcomes resulting from the use of the information presented in this book.

This book is dedicated to:

My Boys

Thank you for always inspiring, loving, and bringing me joy! You are always my inspiration and motivation for everything I do.

"Continued improvement is better than delayed perfection."

– Tony Robbins

CONTENTS

INTRODUCTION

Welcome to a journey of personal transformation!

This book is designed to guide you through key principles that will help you grow, discover your potential, and lead a life of purpose and fulfillment. Every one of us has an incredible ability to evolve, and the process of personal growth is the key to unlocking that power.

Personal growth isn't a destination but a continuous journey—one where we learn, fail, adapt, and thrive. Life will present challenges, but it's in how we respond to these challenges that growth occurs. The chapters in this book are designed to help you embrace that process, starting with an understanding of why personal growth matters.

Each chapter will explore a fundamental aspect of this journey. We'll begin by understanding the importance of growth and how failure, often seen as a setback, is actually one of our greatest teachers. You'll learn to walk your own path without being influenced by the crowds and how to set goals that are specific, measurable, achievable, relevant, and time-bound (SMART). We'll also dive into finding your voice, conducting a personal SWOT analysis to understand your strengths and weaknesses, and the importance of becoming a better listener.

As you progress through the chapters, you'll see the value of making yourself a priority, embracing change, and learning to let go of the things that weigh you down. You'll discover the power of observing yourself without judgment and, finally, how to cultivate the 3 C's: Confidence, Commitment, and Courage, to move forward boldly in life.

This book is not just about self-improvement—it's about self-discovery. It's about learning to embrace every part of your journey, including the failures, the challenges, and the uncertainties, and using them to fuel your growth. By the end of this book, you'll have the tools and insights to lead a more fulfilling, confident, and courageous life.

Let's begin this transformative journey together.

CHAPTER 1

The Importance of Personal Growth

Personal growth is a journey that starts with intention and commitment. Before diving into this transformative path, it's essential to lay a solid foundation by understanding key principles and creating an environment that fosters self-improvement. This initial phase sets the stage for success, ensuring that growth becomes a sustainable and rewarding part of life.

Every meaningful journey begins with a clear intention. Personal growth is no different. It starts with a conscious decision to improve, learn, and evolve. Setting an intention provides focus and purpose, guiding your energy toward self-improvement. Without it, growth can feel scattered and ineffective.

Self-Awareness

In this first chapter of our journey into personal growth, we begin with the essential principle of self-awareness. Understanding yourself is the foundation upon which personal development is built. Here, we will explore what self-awareness truly means, why it is so crucial, and how you can start your own journey of self-discovery.

Self-awareness serves as the compass that guides you on the path of growth. It's about knowing your strengths and weaknesses, understanding your core values and beliefs, and recognizing the emotions and desires that drive you. Gaining insight into what makes you unique, what brings you joy, and what causes stress allows you to build a foundation for intentional personal growth. To start this inner journey, reflect on key questions: What are your core values? What inspires and excites you? What are the sources of dissatisfaction in your life? Knowing these answers forms the basis of self-awareness and sets the stage for change.

A powerful tool in developing self-awareness is self-reflection. It's like looking in a mirror that reveals your thoughts, feelings, and behaviors. Through reflection, you gain valuable insights into who you are and why you act the way you do. This practice can take many forms—journaling, meditation, or even deep conversations with a trusted friend or mentor. The aim is to regularly look inward, observe your thoughts and emotions, and better understand the inner workings of your mind and heart.

Integrating self-reflection into your routine helps shed light on aspects of yourself that may have been hidden. Over time, you'll become more aware of your reactions and feelings, making it easier to face challenges and seize opportunities with greater clarity.

There are several practical exercises you can use to enhance self-awareness. Journaling is a powerful method, helping you track your thoughts and emotions, spot patterns in your behavior, and record personal insights. Regular meditation brings you into the present moment, allowing you to observe your mind without being overwhelmed by it. Seeking feedback from trusted friends or colleagues also offers fresh perspectives on your strengths and areas for growth. Setting aside quiet time for yourself is another way to reflect on your goals and values, providing space to think about the direction of your personal growth. Lastly, using self-assessment tools such as personality tests can offer deeper insight into your strengths and areas where you might improve.

Engaging in these exercises will lead to a more profound understanding of yourself. Remember, self-awareness is not about harsh judgment but about self-acceptance and growth. It involves embracing all aspects of yourself, including your imperfections, and using this awareness to become the best version of you.

As we embark on this journey together, self-awareness will be our guide, illuminating the path ahead. With this understanding, you can make choices that align with your authentic self, setting the stage for deeper personal growth.

Self-awareness is the cornerstone of personal development. Reflecting on your strengths, weaknesses, values, and past experiences offers insight into where you want to improve and excel. This self-reflection acts as a map, showing the path toward growth and helping you understand where to begin.

Once you've reflected on who you are and where you want to go, the next step is defining your goals. These goals, whether short-term or long-term, give direction to your personal growth journey. They should be clear, specific, and aligned with your aspirations. By setting measurable and realistic goals, you can track progress and celebrate each step forward.

Staying motivated is a challenge many face on the road to self-improvement. It's essential to identify what inspires you—whether it's books, mentors, or personal values. Motivation serves as the fuel that keeps you moving forward, especially when challenges arise.

A growth mindset, a concept popularized by Carol Dweck, is a crucial element of self-improvement. Believing that your abilities and intelligence can develop through effort and perseverance opens the door to endless possibilities. With this mindset, you become resilient, ready to face challenges, and eager to learn from mistakes.

The environment around you plays a significant role in personal growth. Surrounding yourself with positive influences and supportive people can enhance your journey, while minimizing negative influences that might hold you back. A nurturing environment helps maintain focus and encourages progress.

Time management is another critical factor in your growth journey. Prioritizing personal development amidst the busyness of life requires careful planning. By allocating time for reflection, learning, and goal-setting, you create a structure that allows growth to flourish.

Accountability can also play a pivotal role in personal growth. Having someone to hold you accountable, whether it's a mentor, coach, or partner, can help you stay on track and committed to your goals. This external support system offers guidance and encouragement as you push forward.

Recognizing and celebrating milestones along the way is vital for maintaining momentum. Small victories affirm that self-improvement is a rewarding endeavor. Each achievement, no matter how small, reinforces your belief in the value of personal growth.

Of course, setbacks are inevitable. The path to self-improvement is rarely linear. However, every setback presents an opportunity to learn and grow. Cultivating resilience in the face of adversity strengthens your ability to keep moving forward, no matter the obstacles.

Setting the stage for self-improvement is a crucial process that lays the groundwork for long-lasting change. With intention, self-reflection, clear goals, and a supportive environment, you create a solid framework for transformative growth. This phase ensures that personal development isn't a fleeting goal but a sustained and enriching journey, preparing you to overcome challenges and unlock your full potential.

Personal growth, also called self-improvement, is about becoming the best version of yourself. It means learning new skills, gaining knowledge, and becoming more self-aware, which all lead to a happier, more fulfilling life. In today's fast-paced world, focusing on personal growth is more important than ever.

A few key points to the why personal growth is important are as follows:

Self-Awareness: The Foundation of Personal Growth

Personal growth starts with self-awareness. This means understanding your strengths, weaknesses, emotions, and values. When you know yourself better, you can make smarter decisions, set goals that matter, and work on areas that need improvement.

The Pursuit of Happiness and Fulfillment

At the heart of personal growth is the search for happiness and fulfillment. Everyone wants to feel content and have a sense of purpose. By working on personal growth, you learn more about who you are, what you love, and what really matters to you. When you live in line with your values and passions, you feel happier and more satisfied with life.

Adapting to Change

In our rapidly changing world, adapting to new situations is key. Personal growth helps you develop the tools and mindset to embrace change instead of fearing it. It teaches you how to be flexible, resilient, and bounce back stronger after setbacks.

Improving Relationships

Personal growth also impacts how you connect with others. As you grow, your emotional intelligence improves, making you more empathetic and compassionate. You become better at understanding other people's feelings and needs, leading to healthier and more meaningful relationships, both personally and professionally.

Better Problem-Solving Skills

Growing as a person helps you develop better problem-solving skills. You become more creative and better equipped to tackle challenges. Whether it's a personal issue or a complex problem at work, personal growth gives you the tools to think critically and find solutions.

Career Success

Personal growth can be a game-changer for your career. By learning new skills and keeping up with industry trends, you can advance in your job or pursue your passions. A growth mindset also helps you stay motivated and reach your professional goals.

Health and Well-Being

Personal growth is closely tied to physical and mental health. It encourages self-care, managing stress, and making healthy choices. When you take care of yourself, you have more energy and motivation to go after your dreams and enjoy life.

Lifelong Learning

Personal growth is also about being a lifetime student. It sparks a desire for knowledge and personal development, which doesn't just benefit you but also impacts those around you. Lifelong learning keeps your mind sharp and opens up new opportunities throughout your life.

The Ripple Effect of Personal Growth

In short, personal growth is a lifelong journey. It's a commitment to becoming the best version of yourself, living with purpose, and staying resilient through life's ups and downs. As you grow, the benefits extend beyond yourself – you positively influence your relationships, your community, and even the world.

Let's Take the Next Step

Now, let's dive deeper into how you can improve various aspects of your life by first focusing on yourself. By working from within, you can create positive changes in every part of your life.

CHAPTER 2

Failure Is Your Best Teacher

"Failure is success in progress."

- Albert Einstein

The best teaching lessons in life come from past failures. Sometimes, people react to their failures as "the end." Instead, it should be seen as a step closer to success. We start something -we make mistakes - then we quit because it didn't work out as we wanted. We think we have failed, which is why most don't even bother to try again. They result in quitting without going back to the drawing board to make their dreams a reality. We all share this common ground of failure. This is when we are presented with two forks in the road: giving up or retrying. Only with our perseverance do we define ourselves as the victims of our failures or become resilient. The resilient mind considers that if our mistakes beat us down, the least we can say is we learned from it.

Are you starting a new relationship, career, or business venture?

Will you give up and stop as soon as something goes wrong? Or will you keep going and take all the lessons from previous experiences to improve and succeed in your next move?

These choices are what determine the outcome of our goals. These are examples of the options life presents us that reveal the essence of our character, drive, and desire toward our objective.

Whatever your failures may be, whether they involve friendships, relationships, or career choices, when *you quit*, then *you have failed.*

Everything we go through teaches us a lesson. Each lesson of life should provide us with a mindset. Humans should always be changing and evolving to a more advanced, progressed, and disciplined sense of self-being, but this is not always true. Sometimes, life tries to teach us something, but when we fail, we see it as "the end." The belief that the first failure determines our outcome can become our crutch. We depend on this as the only option because our defeats do not make us comfortable. When we come to terms with the fact that our failures are unpleasant, it motivates us to relieve that by reattempting, which ultimately leads to success.

The wrong mentality instilled in us, throws us into a negative feedback loop of submission to our insecurities and self-doubt that keeps us going backward. Our hesitations originate from how we perceive and connect to our misfortunes.

Think about a time when you thought you failed at your overall goal. Write it down.

What did you learn from it? Write down at least three things that you learned from that experience.

What are they? How can you implement those lessons in your life right now?

We hang on to negative thoughts and experiences that do not allow us to move forward. If we keep it that way, we either take steps backward or standstill. Either way, we are not moving forward, which means no growth. That is not where we belong - where our process of evolution is at a standstill, and our desire to grow is flooded with self-doubt.

Every day is a new day - you don't look at the calendar and mark off the same day every day, right? We must move forward, one step at a time, one day at a time.

Dropping out of high school was the biggest regret in my life for many years. A self-perception of being inferior to those around me caused self-doubt in my sense of feeling like a good person, mother, and wife. I dropped out of high school at sixteen. My previous years of education were either paused or skipped due to moving many times during my childhood. I was in 6th grade when my parents decided to move to Germany. I started 8th grade over there just a few months later. I finished 8th and 9th grade in Germany .I returned back home at 16 and started High school for only one semester and then I decided to drop out.

Between the gaps in my education and moving to America at just 18 years old, where I had to assimilate into the culture and language and become a first-time mom, my self-doubt greatly strained my self-identity and how I thought others perceived me. At that age, I experienced many life milestones quickly while still trying to grasp my self-view of the world around me. Through all this, the voice of my regret influenced my opinion of myself.

I felt most ashamed when people asked, "Where did you finish school?" I would stare back, pause for a long time, and then answer with half of my voice, "I did not."

As the years went by, my desire to get a full education would still ring in the back of my head. As that ambition grew louder, the more I started to become aware of the opportunities that I had. After some research and drive to find the motivation within myself, suddenly, "my education" was not impossible to achieve. There was still hope.

I know for many people, there may be some surprise or confusion about how I did not register sooner with the ease of the accessible education America has in this era, but it's not as simple as one may think.

First, I didn't have anyone in my inner circle to teach me that. Being in a world surrounded by the fact that no one around me had gone past high school made it a challenge to realize the attainability of my education. Second, I had to work on getting my permanent residency here in the USA for eight years.

When applying for college, if you are not a permanent resident, you are considered an international student. In such cases, tuition prices sometimes triple. Also, I didn't want to start college and suddenly have to leave the country and drop out again.

When you are going through the process in and out of immigration courts, your outcome is unsure, and nothing is certain regarding residency approval. My husband and I came to the U.S. almost sixteen years ago; it took us eight years to receive our permission for residency and fourteen years to become US citizens. It is a long, stressful, time-consuming, and expensive process. However, if you follow all the required steps, it is well worth the work.

Third, I had two kids and no one to watch them. I had to wait until they both started school full-time to be able to start college. I started college in 2012 at my local community college and graduated two years later with my Associates in Liberal Arts and General Business. After that summer, I transferred to another College to get my BA in Business. I finally graduated in June of 2017.

I faced many obstacles during these five years. My life was filled with so many predeterminations not to pursue my goal. I had many reasons to desert my aspiration due to many responsibilities and stressors, which gave me many reasons to throw in the towel.

But I didn't, and I am so grateful that I didn't stop or give up on myself and now have the ambition to inspire others.

Between raising two kids, one miscarriage, and having two more babies, the list is not short of the challenges it took to preserve during those 5 years. But I had an intention - a dream important enough that I concluded that abandoning just wasn't an option. I continued one step at a time (small steps) but kept moving forward, which helped me make it all possible.

Failing was not an option. My past failures had taught me what failure feels like, and it provided the drive not to give up on graduating.

I had given up on my education when I decided to drop out of high school. However, through the years of longing to attain my education, I turned my self-doubt into the courage I needed to jump off the deep end, whether I failed or prevailed. That taught me that no matter what it takes or what you are going through in life- if your goal is important enough, you will find a way to overcome everything life presents you.

When we fail, there is a feeling of not being good enough or smart enough, preventing us from trying again. It hampers our ambitions to give something our full force because we feel like we are undeserving of it due to the previous failure, which leads us not to give it our all and miss out on prime opportunities to fly.

If we let the fear of failure take control of our thoughts, we will do only ordinary things. We will never really go after what we want because the fear of failure controls us. If we look at each failure of our lives as a teaching moment or teaching lesson, we will also get rid of the fear of failure. There is no failure. There are only lessons.

Sometimes, we have people around us (even at a young age) who intentionally or unintentionally instill the fear of failure in us. For me, it was my teacher. As a first-grader, I remember there was a lot of abuse in our classroom school, and it was considered "normal," and in many cases, the parents even encouraged it.

Every day, I remember being horrified to go to school because even though I studied and did all my homework, I was still scared that I would fail and be "punished." So, every single day, I made sure I was prepared for school, yet I entered my classroom with the same anxiety of inferiority and fear of failure.

No child in any part of the world should get up in the morning and go to school horrified from fear that they might fail. Due to the time and place I grew up in, that was the harsh reality of a young student's life. I believe if our teachers and our parents had taught us a different approach to being a good student as well as put into perspective that failing a test or assignment is not the end of the world, certainly, my classmates and I would have entered the classroom with a different feeling. If that were the case, we might have been more excited to learn, and with that, we may have had confidence even if we struggled with a lecture or assignment.

Next time you think of yourself as having failed at something, look at it differently. Learn from it, grow, and keep going.

CHAPTER 3

Follow Your Path - Don't Chase the Crowds

"The one who follows the crowd will usually get no further than the group. The one who walks alone is likely to find himself places no one has ever been." - Albert Einstein

We tend to follow " the group" everywhere we go. The issue is we follow only the crowd that is "around us". We compare our lives to our circle of friends, family, and next-door neighbors. With social media, we have the entire world to analyze ourselves against.

Look at five people you hang out with daily or most of your free time.

Who are they?

What are their fears?

What are their strengths?

What is their background?

What do they do for a living?

What is their religion?

What about their social class?

Are they married?

Do they have kids?

The chances are that you and your close circle have much in common and are very similar in many ways.

When I came to the US, everyone I met or had an opportunity to talk with, I would always ask the same questions, "How many years have you been living here? What do you do for a living?"

I was amazed that everyone had built a great life, worked hard, and bought a house for their family. At that time, all I could think of was, 'When will I have what they have? When will I be able to buy a house for my kids? When am I going to be able to find a job? I was comparing and wanting the same things as the next person. Nothing more. I didn't know there was more, and I didn't realize it was possible to strive further.

As the years went by, I realized that I wanted to finish college to complete my education. I didn't want to get just any job. I wanted a career that I would be happy going to every day.

Had I followed the crowd I was surrounded by, I probably would have never graduated or even started college. My desire to broaden my horizon affected my overall outcome, and without that motive, I would still be influenced by those around me.

At twenty-six, I began my college journey while raising two children. After earning my Associate Degree in General Business and Liberal Arts in 2014, the motivation to pursue my educational path was immense. The same year, I transferred colleges, then had two more boys, and graduated with my BA in June 2017. The laborious sacrifices during the five years of studies were challenging and strenuous, but I would eagerly do it all over again. Looking at the outcome of my quest for achievement, my past struggles and my surroundings became only my fuel to blast off.

In the future, when you find yourself motivated to do something, buy something, or achieve something, first ask yourself, "Do I want it, or do I want it because someone in my circle has it?"

A typical thirty-year-old female has a family or is starting one, maybe has purchased a house, has already finished her education, has a great job, etc. There's nothing wrong with this picture, right? We all might know many people in our circle who have all the above. But there is nothing wrong with being a 30-year-old with no husband, kids, a home mortgage, or even a 9-5 job.

If you choose to pay a mortgage instead of traveling, that is your choice, but if someone else has chosen another path, it does not mean that they are wrong or they are wasting their life. On the contrary, they may be much happier and even more fulfilled.

The way other people perceive others is not necessarily reality. Reality is that you need to follow your path, wherever that might lead you.

It is your choice to make....

Your consequences to pay....

And your lessons to learn...

Again, had I followed people around me, I would have never applied for college. No one in my circle of friends or family, my parents, my husband, or any of the people I met would have given me the ambition

21

to follow my passion. I had no mentor, no support, no advice to take. All I had was my goal to continue my education and choose my career path.

Many people often asked why I was going to college instead of just getting a job. After all, with my husband being the only provider, I agree if I had started working, our lives as a family would have been a little easier. Two paychecks are better than one, after all. The tension between my obligations as a mother and my intention for desired opportunities left me at a crossroads. I could tell that an entry-level job would leave me feeling incomplete. I was aware of my potential, but I could not hear it. My mind was so preoccupied with doubt and external forces that I could not listen to where I needed to go. During this time, I learned that the ability to listen to your inner needs by muting all the negativity would light up the path I need to follow.

If you need support and you get refused, that's okay too. It might take you a little longer, but you will get there. Once you succeed, go even further.

They will doubt, discourage, and even make fun of you, but you can't live, and you should not live your life pleasing people. Making them happy and forgetting about yourself will only cause you to have regrets in your heart and mind.

People are in different stages of their lives. For example, if you and your friend are reading the same book, you just began the story while your friend is well into the sixth chapter. Can you enjoy, understand or appreciate the story/book if you skip to the sixth chapter to keep up with your friend?

Starting from the beginning and reading for yourself is the only way to appreciate and learn from the story.

Even if she tries to summarize what she has learned so far, you won't be able to absorb, welcome, and acknowledge all of the lessons and experiences if you do not immerse and read the book yourself.

Learning comes from experience. It comes from your story. When your story begins, you must start on the first chapter of your journey. You should feel no obligation to skip pages to be where someone else is.

This part of your story should be a process of self-appreciation, self-reflection, and growth. Living your story in someone else's narrative is a disservice to the flourishment already made from your experience. It is an underappreciation of your endurance. By living our truths and ignoring others' perceptions of us, we pay homage to the fact that we have survived what we thought we could not, got up when we have had enough, and stood firm with grace. Finding that voice and searching for the narrative in your story is the first step to letting go and building up.

"Setting goals is the first step in turning the invisible into the visible."

Tony Robbins

CHAPTER 4

Set Smart Goals

In your journey of personal growth, goal setting is the compass guiding you through uncharted waters. By setting clear, meaningful goals using the SMART framework and addressing common obstacles, you'll have a roadmap for the life you want to lead.

Setting the stage for personal growth, the principle of goal setting is a pivotal step in your journey towards self-improvement. It's like charting a course for your life, much like a captain navigating a ship through uncharted waters. In this section, we'll explore the profound significance of clear goals, learn about the SMART goal-setting framework, and discuss common obstacles you might encounter on your path to achieving your dreams.

Imagine you're embarking on a road trip with a clear destination in mind. This journey is an analogy for your life, and the destination represents your goals. Clear goals are your map; they provide direction, purpose, and a sense of achievement.

But goals are not just about reaching a destination; they're about choosing destinations that resonate with your core values and desires. Goals that align with your innermost self become a powerful driving force, motivating you to stretch beyond your comfort zone, learn new things, and overcome challenges. They serve as a source of inspiration, urging you to become the best version of yourself.

When you set meaningful goals, you're setting yourself up for greater success and satisfaction. Achieving these goals can be deeply rewarding, whether they relate to your career, personal relationships, health, or any other aspect of your life. The act of setting and pursuing clear goals keeps you engaged in life and provides a sense of purpose, ultimately enhancing your overall well-being.

Your goals will give you direction, focus, and motivation as you continue to explore, discover, and grow. So, let's set our sights on the future, and take one step closer to the best version of ourselves.

I have always been a planner and have always loved setting goals for myself. But until I learned about goal setting, all my dreams and ideas about what I wanted to do with my life was floating around.

I never wrote anything down and never thought it could make any difference.

I was completely wrong!

When I started to write down my goals and break them into smaller tasks, I immediately saw the difference.

STEP 1- SET SMART GOALS

Setting goals is essential for personal and professional success in today's fast-paced world. However, merely setting goals without a well-defined structure and approach can often lead to vague aspirations or unattainable dreams. That's where the SMART goal framework comes into play.

SMART is an acronym for Specific, Measurable, Achievable, Relevant, and Time-bound.

This framework provides a practical and effective approach to setting clear, realistic, and actionable goals. In this chapter, we will delve into the fundamentals of the SMART goal framework, exploring each component and its significance in creating successful goals. Goal setting is essential for anyone striving for success in any aspect of their lives. Whether it is personal growth, career advancement, or even physical fitness, setting well-defined and meaningful goals is crucial in achieving progress.

However, not all goals are created equal. Many people set vague and uninspiring goals, leading to failure and disappointment.

To set goals that work, you need to use the SMART criteria.

When someone asks you, "What is your goal," how do you answer?

People generally answer with what their dreams are, not what their goals are. Goals are more like stepping stones laid in the ground. If you follow them, a path will lead you where you want to go.

S.M.A.R.T. goals are different from simple goals. They are more substantial and more detailed. They will help create a road map to your success.

Each of these elements is crucial in setting effective goals that are actionable, realistic, and aligned with one's values and aspirations.

S for Specific: The Power of Clarity.

The first element of the SMART goal framework is specificity. Specific goals are clear and well-defined, leaving no room for ambiguity or confusion. When setting specific goals, it is essential to answer the five W's: Who, What, Where, When, and Why. By identifying the key details and defining the goal's scope, individuals clearly understand what they want to achieve.

Specific goals provide a focus and direction, helping individuals prioritize their efforts and allocate resources effectively. For example, instead of setting a general goal like "I want to lose weight," a specific goal would be "I want to lose 10 pounds in three months by exercising for 30 minutes five times a week and following a balanced diet." The specific goal not only outlines the desired outcome but also provides a roadmap for how to achieve it.

Specific goals are those that are clear and unambiguous.

They focus on the outcome or the end result and define what exactly you want to achieve. Make your goal as specific as possible. What exactly are you trying to accomplish? Write down as many details as possible. If you say you want "to be healthy," that is not as specific as "I want to lose 10 pounds." This goal is well-defined, measurable, and has a clear target. It is essential to be clear and straightforward while setting your goal.

Furthermore, specific goals enhance motivation and commitment. When individuals have a clear picture of what they want to accomplish, they are more likely to stay focused and dedicated to their efforts. The clarity of specific goals also enables individuals to track their progress accurately, as they can easily measure their achievements against the defined criteria.

M - Measurability: Tracking progress and staying motivated.

The "M" in the SMART goals acronym stands for Measurable.

Measurability is critical to effective goal setting as it provides a tangible way to track progress and determine success. Individuals can assess their advancements and adjust as needed by establishing specific criteria or metrics that can be quantified. Measurable goals allow for precise evaluation and enable individuals to determine whether they are on track or if modifications are required to achieve their desired outcomes. Additionally, the ability to measure progress provides a sense of motivation and accomplishment as individuals witness their effort translating into measurable results. You should be able to measure and track your progress. Otherwise, how will you know that you have accomplished your goal? Measurable goals can be quantified or tracked to help monitor progress. They give you a clear indication of how far you have come and how much work is left. For instance, instead of setting a goal like "I want to read more books," you could set measurable goals like "I want to read 12 books this year, one book per month."

A - Achievable: Setting realistic and achievable targets.

The "A" in the SMART goals acronym represents Achievable. Setting achievable goals ensures that they are realistic and within reach. It involves assessing one's resources, capabilities, and constraints to determine if the goal can be accomplished. An achievable goal challenges individuals to push their limits and grow, but it also considers the practicality of the goal in relation to their current circumstances.

By setting achievable goals, individuals set themselves up for success rather than setting unrealistic expectations that may lead to frustration or discouragement. This element of the SMART goal framework encourages individuals to balance ambition and feasibility, allowing them to stay motivated and focused on their path to accomplishment.

Is your goal attainable? Achievable goals are challenging but within reach. They take into account your abilities, resources, and constraints. Setting unrealistic or unattainable goals leads to frustration and unmotivation. You must know your limits, circumstances, and resources to achieve this goal. I would like to be taller, but it is not realistic. Make sure your goals are attainable; otherwise, it is just daydreaming in the clouds.

R - Relevance: Aligning goals with personal values and aspirations.

The "R" in the SMART goals acronym stands for Relevant. A relevant goal aligns with an individual's objectives, values, and aspirations. It ensures the goal is meaningful and significant to the individual's personal or professional life.

A relevant goal serves a purpose and contributes to the broader picture of an individual's goal. It is essential to assess the relevance of a goal by considering factors such as the impact it will have, the resources required, and the alignment with one's values and long-term vision. By setting relevant goals, individuals can focus on activities that truly matter to them, increasing motivation and driving meaningful progress. Relevant goals are the ones that align with your values, priorities, and long-term aspirations. They are meaningful and purposeful and contribute to your overall sense of fulfillment, satisfaction, and joy.

Instead of setting a random goal like "I want to learn how to play the piano," you could set a relevant goal like "I want to learn the piano so I can perform at my best friend's wedding." One of my goals is to learn French because I want to spend next summer in France. If I start taking Spanish classes , it won't help me reach my goal. Your steps or action plan must be relevant to your goal and what you are trying to achieve.

T - Time-Bound: Creating deadlines and a sense of urgency.

The "T" in the SMART goals acronym represents Time.

Time-bound goals have a specific deadline or timeframe, creating a sense of urgency and providing a clear target for completion. By setting time-bound goals, individuals are more likely to stay focused, manage their time effectively, and prioritize tasks accordingly. Including a specific timeline helps individuals track their progress and ensures that they are making steady advancements toward their goals. Additionally, time-bound goals allow for better planning and resource allocation, as individuals can set milestones and checkpoints to monitor their progress. By incorporating the element of time into goal setting, individuals can enhance their productivity, maintain momentum, and increase the likelihood of achieving their desired outcomes within a defined timeframe. Time-bound goals are the ones that are tied to a specific deadline or timeframe. They create a sense of urgency and accountability and help you stay on track. For example, instead of setting a goal like "I want to improve my public speaking skills," you could set a time-bound goal like "I want to complete a public speaking course within the next three months and deliver a 10 min speech at the toastmaster club."

There should be a time frame to accomplish your goal. You have to put a due date on it or end up working on it forever. Smart goals can be applied to various areas of our lives, allowing us to set specific, measurable, attainable, relevant, and time-bound goals that drive personal growth and success.

Here are some key areas where SMART goals can be utilized:

Career and Professional Development:

Setting SMART goals in your career can help you advance professionally and achieve success. For example, you can aim to acquire a specific skill or certification within a certain timeframe. This goal would be specific (the skill or certification), measurable (completion or achievement), attainable (feasible within your resources and abilities), relevant (aligned with your career aspirations), and time-bound (within a specified timeframe).

Education and Personal Growth:

SMART goals are highly effective for educational pursuits and personal development. Whether studying for a degree, learning a new language, or developing a new hobby, SMART goals can keep you focused and motivated. For instance, you can set a goal to read a certain number of books within a year, attend a specific number of workshops, or achieve a particular GPA in your studies.

Health and Fitness:

SMART goals can be applied to health and fitness, helping you maintain a healthy lifestyle and achieve your physical well-being objectives. For instance, you can set a goal to exercise a certain number of times per week, reduce your sugar intake, or run a marathon within a specific timeframe. These goals provide clear targets and help you track your progress, keeping you accountable and motivated.

Financial Goals:

SMART goals are invaluable for financial planning and wealth management. Whether you want to save for a down payment on a house, pay off debt, or start a retirement fund, SMART goals can guide your financial decisions. For example, you can set a goal to save a specific amount of money each month, reduce unnecessary expenses, or increase your income by a certain percentage.

Relationships and Social Goals:

SMART goals can also enhance interpersonal relationships and social connections. For instance, you can set a goal to spend quality time with your loved ones, develop better communication skills, or expand your network by attending networking events or joining relevant communities. These goals can foster deeper connections and personal growth in relationships.

Personal Well-being and Self-Care:

Setting SMART goals for personal well-being and self-care is essential for maintaining balance and managing mental and emotional health. You can set goals to practice mindfulness or meditation daily, regularly self-reflect, prioritize self-care activities, or achieve a healthy work-life balance. By applying the SMART framework to these various areas of our lives, we can set meaningful and achievable goals that lead to personal growth, fulfillment, and success. Remember, the key is to ensure that the goals are specific, measurable, attainable, relevant, and time-bound, providing a clear roadmap for progress and achievement in every aspect of our lives.

STEP 2- DIVIDE YOUR END GOAL INTO SMALLER TASKS

Looking at the big picture may be overwhelming and possibly discouraging. Your thoughts may include, "How am I able to achieve that? That is impossible!" But if you divide it into smaller goals or tasks, it doesn't seem so overwhelming.

Going back to my example of getting my degree, I dropped out of high school at sixteen years old, and I began my college journey at twenty-six with two children. If I had just focused on my end goal, without any real plan, I would have come up with a hundred excuses of how my goal is impossible to achieve, and I would have given up before even starting.

Instead, I divided my goal into more practical tasks, and I focused on those.

I like to divide my goals into categories:

- Personal goals
- Professional goals
- Financial goals
- Business goals
- Travel goals

Fun fact: My travel goal list is longer than the other ones.

Some other groups that might be relevant to your goals may be:

- Health & fitness

- Personal growth & development

- Spiritual

- Family

- Social life

- Relationships

I would highly recommend that you start with one category and one goal and then add more as you go along. After you have decided on your category, write down your goal, and apply the SMART method.

STEP 3 - HOLD YOURSELF ACCOUNTABLE

YOU MUST REMIND YOURSELF THAT NO ONE BUT YOU IS RESPONSIBLE FOR YOUR SUCCESS.

IT'S TIME TO PUT A STOP TO EXCUSES LIKE:

- "I CAN'T DO THAT" OR "I DON'T HAVE TIME."

- BLAMING OTHERS

- NEGATIVE THOUGHTS

- NEGATIVITY FROM OTHER PEOPLE

Another suggestion would be finding yourself an accountability partner. An accountability partner is someone that is on the same path as you with the same goals or who loves supporting you no matter what. When I started writing my book, having someone that holds me accountable, and it's on the same path as me, has been really encouraging and helpful.

STEP 4- REWARD YOURSELF

Rewarding yourself for every step you accomplish boosts your confidence with such thoughts like, "I can do this" or " I'm one step closer to reaching my goal." Also, rewarding yourself motivates you and makes all the work even more fun. When I was in college, every semester break, I used to take my boys for a day trip or a long weekend somewhere they liked. I looked forward to spending some quality time with them because I was always studying or doing my homework, even on weekends.

STEP 5- RESTART AND REPEAT- MAKE IT A HABIT

This whole process can be repeated, and every time you do, it is going to be more comfortable and more exciting when you achieve something you are passionate about. When you get overwhelmed working towards your goal, keep in mind,

> "It always seems impossible until it's done."
>
> - Abraham Lincoln

The SMART framework serves as a practical guide for setting goals that are well-structured, focused, and achievable. It helps you clarify your ideas, focus your efforts, and manage your time effectively. By applying these criteria to your goals, you can make your aspirations more tangible and feasible, turning vague dreams into concrete plans for personal growth.

While goal setting is a powerful tool for personal growth, it often comes with challenges. One of the most common obstacles is procrastination. It's easy to delay taking action, but you can overcome this by breaking your goals into smaller, manageable tasks and creating a schedule to tackle them systematically. Fear of failure can also be a significant roadblock, preventing you from setting ambitious goals. The key is to embrace failure as part of the learning process, viewing every setback as an opportunity to grow and improve.

At times, you may experience a lack of motivation. When this happens, it's helpful to revisit your reasons for pursuing the goal. Remind yourself why your goals are important and visualize the benefits of achieving them. Tools like vision boards or journals can keep your motivation alive and strong.

Another challenge is the lack of accountability. Sharing your goals with a trusted friend, family member, or mentor can provide the support and accountability you need to stay on track. They can encourage you and help keep you focused when your commitment wavers.

Setting unrealistic goals is another common issue. If your goals are too ambitious, it can lead to burnout and disappointment. Make sure your goals are challenging but still achievable within your current resources and capabilities.

Lastly, distractions are everywhere in our modern world. Identifying your most significant distractions is key. Once you recognize them, create strategies to minimize their impact. This might involve setting clear boundaries, practicing better time management, or even taking breaks from digital devices to help you focus on your goal pursuit.

CHAPTER 5

Find Your Voice - In Life - At Work- At Home

Finding your voice requires courage, strength, and encouragement. Growing up in a hush-hush culture (mainly around female behavior), I was never allowed to speak up or make independent decisions for myself. Even when I tried, someone older than me would shut me down immediately. Growing up as an only child only caused more difficulty since I had no one to talk to. So, often, I would completely shut down. If I asked, there was no answer. If I spoke, I would be blamed or made fun of. So it was just more comfortable and more convenient not to talk and listen to others and follow their voices and paths.

Feelings of isolation, helplessness, and ostracism can be prevalent when going through this or similar experience. It is only human to react to vulnerability with an attempt to self-soothe. Whether we comply with what other people tell us to do, lash out, or shut-in our lives from the world, we still have the same issue that we haven't confronted. It's easier to not deal with a feeling like this if it is all you have ever known, or maybe you think it is easier to live your life by someone else's voice instead of your own.

The way we take this experience and use it to amplify our voice can result in a positive outcome for what we want our aspirations to be. Sometimes, we even find it very difficult to find our dreams and goals because we are so used to doing what other people tell us we should.

When you continuously have exterior opinions around you that want to make decisions for you with different intentions, the route to the person you want to be or the life you want to have may become blurry. Continual judgment may cause negative reinforcement when making different decisions than those around you. This only feeds the cycle of stagnant self-growth due to the attitudes of those you surround yourself with. Breaking that cycle is the only way to find your true meaning.

Let's dive deeper by reflecting on a time in your life when you felt unheard or voiceless. This is a powerful exercise that can help you reclaim your voice and empower your journey. To begin, let's create a mind map to organize your thoughts visually and make sense of your emotions. Use the following prompts to guide your reflection:

- What was the experience that made you feel voiceless?

- Who or what caused this experience?

- How has this experience impacted your life?

- How did it make you feel?

- What do you want to change about this experience?

Now, let's elaborate further. Why did it make you feel this way?

Understanding the emotions tied to your experience is crucial for healing. Consider how these feelings have shaped your identity and how they influence your current actions.

Next, reflect on the origin of the cause. Where did it come from? What were the circumstances surrounding this experience? How did it happen? Analyzing the context can provide insights into patterns that may have developed over time. This is an opportunity to reassess your beliefs and the narratives you have internalized.

Think about the new things you would like to learn about yourself, as a result of this reflection. What insights can you gain that will help you grow and evolve? Consider what bad habits you want to quit, that may have been acquired from this experience. Are there behaviors or thought patterns that no longer serve you, rooted in feelings of powerlessness or self-doubt?

In this process, identify what the experience has taught you. What lessons can you extract from the pain or struggle? Are there strengths you discovered within yourself during this time? Embrace the knowledge gained and think about what you can leave behind. Letting go of negativity associated with this experience is crucial for moving forward.

Creating a clear structure around your feelings and brainstorming all aspects of how this issue occurred is a vital step toward finding your voice. This reflective exercise not only helps you articulate your thoughts but also serves as a form of emotional healing. By providing clarity and understanding to what happened, you can clear your path to success.

Remember, this journey of self-exploration and healing is not just about the past; it's about forging a new path forward. By addressing these questions and confronting your feelings, you empower yourself to speak up, assert your needs, and embrace your true potential.

Granting yourself access to your expression is a strength that can allow you to make your mark on the world around you. In finding your voice, your power begins to outnumber your fears. Overcoming will be the motivation you need to heal yourself so you can achieve the success you were meant to have. To find your expression, you can put your life in terms of a flower. A flower doesn't bloom or wither away because someone is looking at it or approves of it. It blooms because that is what it was meant to do. The same goes for a happy future. Your life shouldn't flourish based on the opinion of others. Your success should be defined by the act of your prosperity, being something you were meant to do. The moment you decide to spend your life by doing and not seeking is the only moment you can unlock your full potential.

Sometimes, living through the voices of other people's opinions for so long gives us a sense of comfortability. We become so voiceless; we forget we have one ourselves. Putting that voice to use after living with the intentions that aren't yours can cause great difficulty in every aspect of your life. Finding that confidence inside yourself will take time. Ironically, it is a journey you take on your own. Choosing your own time and space to do so is an essential factor in creating your individuality. It may be hard, but it will be worth it.

Finding the courage to overcome the challenges around you is not easy, but it can be done step by step. It's up to you to summon the bravery to find your voice. One small way to start is by speaking up for yourself, even if you feel unsure. These moments can remind you of the strength you've always had inside, which may have been drowned out by others. Once you listen to that voice and make choices for yourself, the possibilities become limitless.

CHAPTER 6

Do a Swot Analysis on Yourself

A SWOT analysis—short for Strengths, Weaknesses, Opportunities, and Threats—is a tool commonly used in business to evaluate a company's position and strategy. It helps organizations identify where they excel, where they need improvement, the opportunities they can seize, and the threats they must address. However, this powerful tool can also be adapted for personal growth, allowing you to gain deeper insights into your life and choices.

Conducting a personal SWOT analysis is a way to reflect on your current situation and clarify your path forward. It encourages self-awareness by helping you identify your personal strengths and weaknesses, while also pinpointing opportunities for growth and obstacles you may face.

This exercise not only increases self-awareness but also empowers you to make informed decisions about your future. By understanding where you stand now, you can begin shaping the direction you want to take. Let's explore each part of the SWOT analysis and how you can apply it to your personal life.

Strengths: What Are Your Strengths?

Your strengths are the unique qualities that set you apart. Everyone has something they excel at, whether it's a particular skill, mindset, or life experience. Identifying your strengths can be an empowering way to boost confidence and focus on areas where you naturally shine. Ask yourself the following:

- What are you good at? Think about your core skills, both technical and personal. These could range from problem-solving to creativity, leadership, or even empathy.

- What is your expertise? Are there areas where you are particularly knowledgeable or experienced?

- What do you enjoy doing? Sometimes what you love to do also reflects your strengths. Passion often fuels excellence.

- Are you trustworthy? Dependable? A good listener? Personal attributes like these can be major strengths in relationships and work environments. - What are your advantages? This could be your education, your network, or even certain resources like time and energy that you have available to invest in yourself.

- What life experiences have shaped you? Unique experiences, whether positive or challenging, contribute to your strength and resilience.

By identifying your strengths, you're better equipped to leverage them in your personal and professional life. These strengths can serve as a foundation for pursuing opportunities and achieving success.

Weaknesses: What Are Your Weaknesses?

Understanding your weaknesses is key to personal growth. It allows you to recognize where you might need to put in extra effort, seek help, or develop new skills. Weaknesses are not limitations but areas of potential improvement. Consider the following:

- Do you have habits that hold you back? Whether it's procrastination, a lack of organization, or other negative patterns, identifying them is the first step toward changing them.

- Do you struggle with self-doubt? Lack of confidence can prevent you from taking action. It's important to acknowledge this so you can work on building self-belief.

- What are your fears? Fear of failure, fear of rejection, or fear of change are common, but confronting them can open doors to personal growth. - Are there areas where you lack knowledge or skills? Be honest about where you need more training, education, or practice.

- Do you avoid challenges? Weaknesses often stem from avoiding difficult situations or tasks. Growth requires stepping outside your comfort zone.

Facing your weaknesses head-on is crucial. Once identified, you can work on strategies to overcome them—whether it's through learning, seeking mentorship, or building confidence in areas where you feel unsure.

Opportunities: What Opportunities Are Available to You?

Opportunities are the external factors that you can take advantage of to improve your situation, achieve your goals, or accelerate your growth. Often, they arise when you turn your strengths into action or overcome your weaknesses. Here are some questions to consider:

- What positive changes could you make in your life right now? Are there habits you could form, skills you could learn, or connections you could build?

- How can you improve your current situation? Is there something you've been wanting to try or pursue that could lead to personal growth? - What strengths could open doors for you? Think about how you could use your talents or expertise to create new opportunities—whether in your career, relationships, or hobbies.

- Is there a gap or need you can fill? Sometimes opportunities lie in recognizing a need that hasn't been addressed—whether it's in your community, workplace, or even within yourself.

- What external trends or changes could benefit you? Opportunities can also come from societal changes, technological advancements, or cultural shifts. How can you position yourself to take advantage of them?

The key to maximizing opportunities is staying open to change and being proactive. Opportunities don't always knock on your door—you have to create or seek them out.

Threats: What Threats Could Hold You Back?

Threats are the external factors that could hinder your progress or personal development. While opportunities represent potential benefits, threats represent the challenges or risks that could disrupt your growth. To navigate these, you need to be aware of what could stand in your way:

- What obstacles are currently in your path? These could be anything from time constraints, lack of resources, financial difficulties, or even conflicting commitments.

- Are you facing competition? Whether it's in your career or personal life, competition for resources, attention, or opportunities can pose a challenge. - Are there changes on the horizon? Big changes—such as shifts in your industry, moving to a new city, or personal life changes—can create uncertainty and obstacles.

- Do you have obligations that might limit your time or focus? These could be personal responsibilities like caring for family or professional obligations that take up more time than you'd like.

By identifying potential threats, you can prepare for them. Knowing what could go wrong allows you to develop strategies to manage risks and turn challenges into opportunities for growth.

Putting It All Together: Your Personal SWOT Strategy

After completing your personal SWOT analysis, take a step back and reflect on your findings. The goal is to create a balanced view of yourself, acknowledging both your strengths and weaknesses while recognizing the opportunities you can seize and the threats you need to overcome.

- Leverage your strengths: Use them to maximize opportunities and address weaknesses.

- Work on your weaknesses: Identify one or two key areas for improvement and create a plan to address them.

- Seize opportunities : Take action on opportunities that align with your strengths and goals.

- Mitigate threats: Develop strategies to manage or avoid the threats in your life, turning challenges into learning experiences.

Your personal SWOT analysis can become a roadmap for growth. By regularly revisiting and updating it, you'll stay attuned to changes in yourself and your environment, and you'll be better equipped to adapt, thrive, and achieve your personal goals.

By doing a SWOT analysis on yourself, you gain clarity on where you stand and what actions you need to take to move forward. It's not just about highlighting strengths or identifying weaknesses—it's about using this knowledge as a powerful tool for personal transformation. Keep this analysis as part of your self-reflection routine, and watch as it helps you navigate your personal growth journey.

CHAPTER 7

Become a Better Listener

"Most people do not listen with the intent to understand;
they listen with the intent to reply."

- Stephen Covey

We listen with the intent to reply and give our opinion when we start a conversation. I think our responses would be very different if we stopped thinking about what we are going to respond with and instead truly listen to the other person.

Sometimes, we assume where the conversation is going and immediately cut off the conversation and reply, even though we may not fully understand what the other person was trying to say. Cutting people off shows a lack of respect for the other side of the conversation's feelings and opinions. Plus, if we fail to let the full point of view and notion naturally flow through the conversation, the premature reaction could even cause an argument because the other person meant something else and you interpreted it differently.

If we take the time to listen, sometimes a reply is not as necessary as we think and may not even be asked for. People want to be heard. They want to be able to express themselves without having an answer from another point of view. When their feelings get counteracted with another person's opinion, it makes the person feel invalid compared to the other side of the conversation.

How does being a good listener help you grow as a person?

It helps you in many ways. If you are a good listener, that means that you care and you empathize.

When we have a higher self-awareness of our own words and actions, we realize how they affect others. Self-awareness provides us with stable confidence in our own feelings, which can help validate the feelings of others. Therefore, this balanced self-esteem helps us become the type of listener that we want in other people during our times of self-expression.

Being a good listener helps you build positive relationships in life, career, relationships, and friendships.

You can become a better listener by:

- Practicing mental stillness

- Making remarks or opinions only when positive or necessary

- Thinking before responding

- Remembering that listening is a win/win

- Being attentive and respectful to others ideas, opinions and emotions

- Being present

- Showing empathy

- Practicing open-mindedness

You will have a higher emotional intelligence when practicing these healthy habits. Our emotional intelligence is the awareness of our emotions and the emotions of those around us. If we put it into perspective that these are small practices that we should already be integrating into our common daily courtesies, it makes it easier to achieve becoming a better listener without having to feel we're striving for it.

We have to be okay with not being comfortable. There may be times in your life where you will hear stories that you might not like and opinions that you might not agree with. Unfortunately, not every single person we talk to has a great happy story to tell us.

When my friend first told me about the abusive relationship she was living in, at first, I honestly didn't want to know. I was not comfortable listening to her due to the thought of how difficult her situation was. At some point during that conversation, I had to stop listening to her. I wished she didn't tell me her story due to the helplessness I felt.

After all, what was I able to do? How was I able to help her?

It is easier for us not to deal with difficult issues. But we need to get out of our comfort zone. If we want people to listen to our difficult, painful stories, then we need to listen to others.

Thinking back now, I wish I had been more empathetic and understanding towards her. After she told me the first time, I didn't want to bring back the conversation because it was too uncomfortable for me.

We can't close our ears and eyes when conversations get too uncomfortable. As a friend and as a woman, one thing I could do is listen even if I don't have any advice to give back or any way to help. A lot of times, our mere presence can be the support someone needs during their time of struggle.

In many cases, we don't have any power to change people's situations, but we do have the ability to listen and be understanding. That is sometimes the greatest help of all.

Try to be a better listener because:

- People want and need to be heard.

- By being an active listener, you will learn more about the other person and understand what they are trying to communicate.

- You develop patience, which is very difficult to learn but a precious virtue to have.

- It shows the real strength and self-control you possess.

- You become more compassionate and understandable.

- It improves relationships and earns trust.

- It benefits problem-solving.

- It provides mutual trust in conversations.

- It provides respect and confidence for both sides of the discussion.

When listening, avoid doing the following:

- Jumping to conclusions

- Missing the point

- Creating unnecessary hostile environments

- Lashing out when in disagreement

- Providing your opinions or stories that revolve around you when people open up to you.

Becoming the listener we want in other people listening to us assists in setting aside our ego and choosing a selfless input into the lives of other people. To achieve this, we must set simple principles for ourselves in the way we act daily. Becoming a better listener provides us with an unbiased goal set to chase our success further.

"The art of conversation lies in listening."

- Malcolm Forbes

CHAPTER 8

Make Yourself a Top Priority- Self Care

The principle of self-care is a crucial juncture on our journey of personal growth. In the relentless pursuit of self-improvement and actualization, it's easy to overlook the importance of self-care. However, it is the foundation upon which all other principles stand. This chapter delves into the profound significance of prioritizing your well-being, the different types of self-care, and strategies for achieving balance between self-care and other responsibilities.

Self-care is not selfish; it's a self-preserving act that empowers you to be your best self in all aspects of your life. As you continue your journey of personal growth, remember that taking care of yourself is a vital foundation for achieving your goals and becoming the person you aspire to be.

Before you can effectively care for others, you must prioritize taking care of yourself. Self-care is sometimes misunderstood as selfishness, but in reality, it's the foundation for being able to give more to those around you. By nurturing your mental and physical well-being, you create the energy, resilience, and motivation needed to fulfill your responsibilities and support others. Practicing self-care is vital for maintaining your overall health and boosting your self-confidence. When you feel balanced and energized, you're better equipped to make sound decisions and stay productive.

So, let's celebrate self-care as a cornerstone of well-being and use it as a springboard to reach new heights in our pursuit of self-improvement.

So, how can we practice self-care?

The first step is learning how to rest, both physically and mentally. Burnout is all too common, and I've experienced it many times throughout my life. It creeps in when we don't recognize the importance of pausing and recharging. When we constantly push ourselves without taking breaks, our energy, focus, and motivation gradually diminish until there's nothing left to give.

Our bodies and minds reach a breaking point when they're overwhelmed by the demands of daily life—whether it's work, relationships, or endless responsibilities. The weight becomes unbearable, and eventually, we hit a wall of exhaustion. We find ourselves burned out, unable to move forward, and in the worst cases, we quit entirely. It's like an electrical fuse that blows when overloaded; once it's been pushed too far, it shuts down. The same happens to us when we ignore the signs of burnout—we shut down mentally, physically, and emotionally, abandoning the goals we've worked so hard to achieve.

To prevent this, we must consciously address the sources of our stress and make time to recharge. Identifying where the pressure is coming from—whether it's work, family obligations, or self-imposed expectations—is crucial for finding balance. Taking care of both our mental and physical health is not a luxury; it's a necessity for living a successful, fulfilled life. A healthy mind fosters a productive, successful life, while neglecting self-care often leads to setbacks and frustration.

You may have heard the phrase, "You can't pour from an empty cup." This principle rings true in every aspect of life. When you're drained and depleted, there's simply nothing left to give—not to your work, your loved ones, or even to yourself. Trying to push forward without rest and replenishment will only lead to more burnout, making success feel out of reach. But when you prioritize your well-being, everything shifts. You regain energy, clarity, and focus, allowing you to give your best to both your personal and professional life.

Self-care isn't just about the physical—it's mental, emotional, and spiritual, too.

Mental self-care involves taking time to rest your mind, finding moments of peace through practices like meditation or mindfulness.

In the realm of mental self care, positive thinking stands as a guiding principle, illuminating the path to self-improvement. It's about harnessing the power of your thoughts and beliefs to shape a brighter, more fulfilling future.

As we continue on this chapter to explore the significance of positive thinking, how to cultivate a positive mindset, offer strategies for managing negative self-talk, and opening the door to the transformative world of positivity.

Positive thoughts act like seeds planted in the rich soil of your mind. When nurtured, they grow into a flourishing garden of personal growth and well-being. These thoughts have the power to shape your reality, influence your actions, and impact the world around you. The connection between the mind and body is profound—positive thinking can reduce stress, improve your immune system, and enhance your overall quality of life. Research consistently shows that those who maintain a positive outlook experience better physical and emotional well-being.

Positive thoughts also build mental resilience. They help you cope with stress, bounce back from setbacks, and maintain a balanced perspective even in difficult times. When you focus on positivity, you cultivate an inner strength that allows you to navigate life's ups and downs with grace. Moreover, the Law of Attraction suggests that focusing on positive thoughts can draw more positivity into your life, creating a cycle of optimism and abundance. Positive thinking not only opens your mind to new possibilities but also enhances your problem-solving abilities. Approaching challenges with an optimistic mindset allows you to find solutions more easily and to overcome obstacles that might otherwise seem insurmountable.

Self-confidence is another key outcome of positive thinking. When you believe in yourself and your abilities, you are more likely to take on new challenges and pursue your goals. This belief in your potential fuels personal growth, allowing you to achieve more than you thought possible.

Cultivating a positive mindset doesn't mean ignoring life's difficulties or adopting a naïve outlook. It's about choosing to focus on solutions, opportunities, and the bright side of life, even when faced with adversity. One effective way to foster a positive mindset is to practice gratitude.

Regularly acknowledging the good things in your life—whether small or large—helps shift your focus from what's lacking to what's abundant. Keeping a gratitude journal can be a powerful tool for maintaining this practice.

Another way to nurture positivity is by consciously shifting your perspective. When faced with a negative situation, look for the lesson or silver lining. This shift in outlook can transform how you see challenges, helping you approach them with a more optimistic mindset. At the same time, it's important to challenge any limiting beliefs you hold. These negative thoughts often stand in the way of personal growth, but by questioning their validity and replacing them with empowering beliefs, you can reshape your mindset.

Affirmations are another tool that can reinforce a positive self-image. By repeating affirmations daily, you remind yourself of your worth and potential, building a stronger foundation of self-belief. Surrounding yourself with positive influences is equally crucial. Spend time with people who uplift and inspire you, and avoid environments that drain your energy or foster negativity.

Visualization is another powerful technique for cultivating a positive mindset. By picturing yourself achieving your goals and experiencing success, you align your thoughts with the emotions of fulfillment and joy. This mental rehearsal strengthens your belief in your ability to turn those visualizations into reality.

Positive thinking is not just a fleeting state of mind; it is a transformative force that, when consistently practiced, can reshape your life. It enhances your resilience, creativity, self-confidence, and ability to navigate the complexities of life. When you embrace the power of positive thinking, you lay the groundwork for personal growth, enabling you to move forward with confidence, clarity, and optimism.

Emotional self-care requires acknowledging your feelings and working through them in a healthy way.

Spiritual self-care is about connecting to something larger than yourself, whether through religious practices, nature, or simply through reflection and meditation.

Here are some simple ways to practice self-care:

- Meditating to calm and center your mind. One of my favorite meditation techniques is "the 6 phase meditation" by Vishen Lakhiani

- Doing yoga to enhance both flexibility and mindfulness

- Spending quality time with loved ones

- Treating yourself to a relaxing spa day

- Going for walks, whether alone for solitude or with others for connection

- Establishing a routine to help you manage your tasks more efficiently - Maintaining a regular exercise routine and a healthy diet

- Getting enough sleep and waking up early to carve out personal time

- Taking short breaks throughout the day—even five-minute breaks can make a big difference

- Saying "no" when necessary to protect your energy

- Staying organized and decluttering, as a messy environment can add unnecessary stress

- Reading books that bring you joy or inspire you

Indulging in activities that nourish your soul not only boosts your mood but also enhances your productivity. Taking time to care for yourself—mentally, physically, and emotionally—will leave you better equipped to tackle your daily challenges. In fact, it's far more efficient to make time for yourself each day than to try and care for others when you're already depleted. Your success is directly linked to your emotional, physical, and mental well-being.

By putting self-care first, you'll build the confidence to face each day, step by step, with renewed energy and focus. When you invest in your well-being, you are also investing in your future success. Self-care lays the foundation for resilience, mental clarity, and emotional strength—cornerstones of personal growth and fulfillment.

Here's why prioritizing well-being is not a luxury but a necessity:

1. Physical Health: Taking care of your body ensures you have the energy and vitality to pursue your goals and dreams. Good physical health is essential for your overall well-being.

2. Mental Clarity: A well-rested and healthy mind is more effective in problem-solving, decision-making, and learning. Mental well-being is essential for personal growth.

3. Emotional Resilience: Emotional well-being allows you to navigate life's ups and downs with grace. It enables you to manage stress, cultivate positive relationships, and persevere in the face of adversity.

4. Balance: Prioritizing well-being helps you strike a balance between work, personal life, and your self-improvement journey. It prevents burnout and promotes long-term consistency.

5. Self-Reflection: Self-care provides the space for self-reflection, helping you gain insight into your needs, desires, and values. This self-awareness is a crucial element of personal growth.

6. Stress Reduction: Taking time for self-care helps reduce stress, which can otherwise hinder your progress. A stress-free mind is more open to creativity and personal development.

7. Quality Relationships: When you prioritize your well-being, you are better equipped to engage in healthy and fulfilling relationships with others. Your self-care influences how you interact with and support those around you.

Ultimately, self-care is a form of self-love that not only elevates your own life but also strengthens your ability to positively impact those around you.

It's an essential ingredient in your journey toward success and fulfillment.

CHAPTER 9

Embrace Change

"If it doesn't challenge you, it does not change you."

- Fred DeVito.

Take a moment to assess where you are in life and where you truly want to be. If you're not satisfied with your current situation, it's time to make a change. However, change often brings challenges. For instance, if you're unhappy with your job, improving your situation might require pursuing further education or leaving your current position to seek new opportunities. This can be daunting, as it involves considering factors like expenses, time, and other responsibilities. These obstacles may make your goal seem out of reach, but gathering the courage to push through will reward you immensely. Leaving your comfort zone is difficult, but if you learn to embrace the challenge as part of the journey, it won't feel so impossible.

Many people hesitate to take that leap because of fear. If you never challenge yourself, you'll remain stuck in the same cycle, repeating the same patterns. Growth only happens when we push beyond our comfort zone, but that zone can feel so cozy that change seems unnecessary. You might have a nice home, a good car, and a well-paying job—things that many people dream of. But if you dread going to work every day, what's the point?

You start each morning rushing to work, dealing with traffic, and spending your day in a job you don't enjoy, surrounded by people you don't connect with. After a long day, you come home exhausted, but you still have other responsibilities—your spouse needs your attention, your kids are eager to spend time with you. By the time you finally settle in, it's time to go to bed and repeat the same routine the next day. The same job, the same frustrations, and the same guilt about not having enough time for your family. It becomes a cycle that feels never-ending.

Or, you could challenge yourself to make a change. You could switch careers, pursue a higher education, or even start your own business. Anything is possible when you embrace the challenge and give yourself the opportunity to grow. Facing challenges head-on means you're not afraid to move forward, even when the path is difficult.

Change is an inevitable part of life, but how we approach it determines our growth. We need to practice viewing change as an opportunity rather than something to fear. Without change, progress is impossible. If you don't choose to advance, nothing in your life will shift. The greatest challenge we face is embracing change, but it's through change that we grow. When you believe in your ability to thrive and evolve in any situation, you've already won the battle. You've already succeeded.

Adaptability is a pivotal waypoint in our quest for personal growth. In a world marked by constant change and uncertainty, adaptability is the skill that empowers us to navigate the shifting sands of life. Learning to adapt not only strengthens our resilience but also opens doors to endless opportunities that might otherwise remain closed.

Life's unpredictability can feel daunting, but it's also the source of growth and opportunity. Whether in your personal relationships, career, health, or the world at large, the ability to navigate change and uncertainty is essential for personal development. Change, when embraced, becomes a gateway to growth and discovery. But to harness its full potential, we must learn to adapt.

Here's why adaptability is crucial:

1. Resilience: Adaptability and resilience go hand in hand. When you're adaptable, you're more capable of bouncing back from setbacks. Resilience is not about avoiding failure, but about learning from challenges and maintaining a positive outlook even when the future feels uncertain.

2. Continuous Learning: Adaptability encourages a mindset of continuous learning. By embracing new experiences and environments, you open yourself up to new skills, knowledge, and perspectives—key components of personal growth.

3. Problem-Solving: When you are adaptable, you can approach problems from a fresh angle. Change forces us to think creatively and find innovative solutions to unexpected challenges.

4. Embracing Opportunities: Adaptable individuals are open to seizing new opportunities, even when they arise unexpectedly. This proactive attitude can lead to personal and professional advancement.

5. Enhanced Creativity: Adaptability fosters creativity. When you're not afraid of change, you allow yourself to think outside the box, explore new ideas, and experiment with new solutions.

6. Improved Relationships: Being adaptable improves your relationships because it enables you to navigate changes in others' lives and meet them where they are. It allows for compromise, understanding, and emotional flexibility, which are essential for fulfilling connections.

7. Reduced Stress: Resisting change is exhausting. When you embrace adaptability, you lower your stress levels because you're less likely to feel overwhelmed by the shifting nature of life. Instead of resisting, you go with the flow, knowing that change can lead to new and better things.

Adaptability is not an inherent trait, but a skill that can be developed with practice and intention. Like any other skill, the more you work on it, the better you become. To cultivate adaptability, start by adopting a growth mindset. This involves believing that your abilities and intelligence can grow with effort and perseverance. When you face challenges, see them as opportunities to learn and improve, rather than obstacles to fear.

Embracing change is another crucial step. Instead of avoiding the unfamiliar, actively seek out new experiences and opportunities that challenge you to think differently. The more you expose yourself to new environments and ideas, the more comfortable you'll become with change. Resilience also plays a key role in adaptability. Learning to bounce back from adversity, whether through mindfulness, meditation, or simply focusing on what you can control, strengthens your ability to adapt in the face of uncertainty.

Reflecting on past experiences is an excellent way to learn how to handle future changes. Look back at how you've navigated challenges in the past—what did you learn, and how did those experiences shape you? This reflection will provide valuable insights that you can carry into future situations. Seeking feedback from those around you is equally important. Constructive criticism can help you identify areas where you need to be more flexible and open to new approaches.

To be truly adaptable, you must remain open-minded. Engage with perspectives and ideas that may seem unfamiliar or uncomfortable at first. Expanding your thinking allows you to be more receptive to change and helps you adjust more easily when needed. It's also important to set realistic expectations. Recognize that not everything will go as planned, and be prepared to adjust your goals or approach as circumstances evolve.

A strong support system is invaluable when navigating change. Surround yourself with people who encourage your growth and offer advice or comfort during uncertain times. Having a network of trusted individuals can provide the emotional and practical support you need to stay grounded.

Another critical aspect of adaptability is stepping outside your comfort zone. Personal growth often happens when we push ourselves beyond what feels safe or familiar. Regularly engaging in activities that challenge your assumptions will help you become more adaptable over time.

Flexibility is key. Agility in your thinking and actions allows you to pivot when needed without losing sight of your long-term goals. Along with that, taking care of yourself is essential. Adaptability requires energy and mental clarity, which can be sustained through proper self-care—ensuring you get enough sleep, exercise, and manage stress effectively.

In today's rapidly changing world, keeping up with technology is also a part of adaptability. Staying informed about new tools and digital advancements will enable you to navigate changes in both your personal and professional life more effectively.

By working on these aspects, you can develop the adaptability necessary to thrive in a world that is constantly evolving. The ability to embrace change, remain flexible, and continually grow will allow you to face life's challenges with confidence and resilience.

Transforming Change into Opportunity

Change doesn't have to be something we merely survive—it can be something we thrive on. When you start to see change as an opportunity for growth, everything shifts. You realize that every new situation, no matter how difficult, brings with it the potential for transformation. Instead of asking, "Why is this happening to me?" start asking, "What can I learn from this?"

As you continue your journey of self-improvement, remember that adaptability is your most potent ally. It's the key to unlocking your full potential, no matter what life throws at you. When you master the ability to adapt, you become unstoppable—not because life suddenly becomes easy, but because you've learned to thrive in the midst of change.

Embracing change is a mindset. It's about welcoming the unknown with curiosity rather than fear, and recognizing that within every challenge lies the seed of opportunity. By developing the skills to navigate uncertainty, you not only prepare yourself for future challenges but also open yourself up to unexpected joys and successes along the way.

So, let's celebrate adaptability as a superpower that empowers us to master the dynamic world we live in and become the best versions of ourselves.

CHAPTER 10

Let Go of Things That Hold You Down

We can't grow as individuals when we have countless things holding us back from moving forward. Some of these barriers are ones we're aware of, while others may go unnoticed. Fear kept me from pursuing my goals for years. If I had known how to overcome that fear earlier, I might have started college much sooner.

Our first step into freeing ourselves from oppressive baggage is to assess what we need to let go of and what is holding us back. Acknowledging your issue or pain and moving on is the only way to strive forward. Otherwise, you are only going to regress to a state of mind that will not benefit your happiness or success.

Here are a few key examples of what may be holding you back:

HAVING A CLOSED MENTALITY

Becoming more open-minded to everything that comes into your life is the key to becoming a more understanding person. Having a closed-minded mentality will only limit you from seeing other people's perceptions. These perceptions can be beautiful lessons to integrate into your own life. They can help you grow as well as take into consideration the growth of others. Usually, closed-minded people are stubborn, and it is complicated to have disagreements with them. They don't like doing things differently or listen to new ideas. We are all naturally predisposed to having a closed mindset to keep ourselves emotionally protected. But our openness can define our inner truth, and without taking external considerations into our lives, we may never find the truth we all seek.

NEGATIVE SELF-TALK

To begin managing negative self-talk, the first step is to identify your negative thought patterns. Pay attention to the recurring thoughts or beliefs that tend to hold you back. Once you become aware of these patterns, you can begin to address them more effectively.

When a negative thought surfaces, it's important to challenge it. Ask yourself whether this thought is grounded in facts or if it's based on assumptions. Often, you'll find that negative self-talk isn't rooted in reality. Look for evidence that contradicts the thought and provides a more balanced perspective.

As you challenge these negative thoughts, work on replacing them with positive affirmations. For instance, if you find yourself thinking, "I'll never succeed," consciously counter it with, "I am capable of achieving my goals." Over time, this practice will help rewire your mindset toward a more constructive outlook.

Practicing self-compassion is also key to breaking the cycle of negative self-talk. Treat yourself with the same kindness you would offer a friend. Understand that no one is perfect, and making mistakes is part of being human. Forgive yourself for your imperfections and move forward with empathy and patience.

Finally, don't hesitate to seek support when needed. Sharing your thoughts and feelings with a trusted friend, family member, or therapist can provide valuable perspective. They can help you recognize when your self-talk is overly critical and offer encouragement as you work to shift it in a positive direction.

RESENTMENT/GRUDGES

The sooner you forgive, the better it is for you and your inner peace. It is only human to struggle with forgiveness. It's an uphill battle that can make or break a person. Recognizing the difference between being a victim or a survivor of your troubles is the first step to having control of this remission.

Letting go of blame—whether it's directed at yourself or others—is an important step toward achieving a healthier mindset. This doesn't mean forgetting what happened or excusing someone's actions. Instead, it's about recognizing that holding onto blame only drains you, emotionally, mentally, and even physically, without offering anything in return. Blame acts like a parasite, feeding off your energy and taking away from your well-being. The key to overcoming it is to focus on your resilience each day, reminding yourself of your strength rather than what or who wronged you.

The next step is forgiveness. Often, we hold onto grudges because we feel justified when the other party doesn't show remorse. However, forgiveness isn't about them—it's about freeing yourself. Forgiving allows you to honor your own journey and release the hold that past pain has over you. As Mahatma Gandhi wisely said, "The weak can never forgive. Forgiveness is the attribute of the strong." By embracing forgiveness, you empower yourself to choose the person you want to become and grow beyond your struggles.

TOXIC RELATIONSHIPS

Toxic relationships can exist in any area of your life—whether it's a friendship, a romantic partner, a family member, or even a colleague. Recognizing when a relationship is negatively affecting your well-being is crucial for your mental and emotional health. Some individuals may unintentionally drain your energy, constantly pulling you down with their negativity or neediness. While you might feel sympathy for their struggles, it's not your responsibility to rescue them from their own toxicity. Your first priority should always be taking care of yourself, just as it is their responsibility to manage their own behavior and emotions.

Acknowledging that a relationship is harmful is the first step toward change.

You don't need to confront the person with hostility or engage in arguments. Instead, you can choose to distance yourself and set boundaries that protect your peace. This can be especially difficult when the person involved is a spouse or close family member, but ultimately, you are responsible for your own life and happiness. It's important to remember that staying in a relationship that makes you miserable won't make anyone truly happy—not even the person you're trying to please.

Detoxifying your relationships may require hard decisions, but those decisions will pave the way for healthier connections and greater personal growth. Surround yourself with people who uplift and support you, rather than those who drain your energy or perpetuate negativity. You deserve to thrive, and maintaining toxic relationships only holds you back from achieving your fullest potential. In the end, prioritizing your well-being isn't selfish—it's necessary for your personal growth and happiness.

WORRYING

Worrying is one of the most common mental habits that can hold you back. While it's natural to have concerns about the future, constant worry can become paralyzing, preventing you from taking action and living fully in the present. Worry often focuses on things that are out of your control—things that might never happen or situations you can't change. When you allow worry to dominate your thoughts, it consumes your energy and keeps you stuck in a loop of fear and doubt.

The key is to understand that worrying doesn't solve problems—it only magnifies them in your mind. It tricks you into believing that by obsessing over every detail, you can somehow prevent negative outcomes, but in reality, it only leaves you feeling drained and overwhelmed. You spend so much time imagining worst-case scenarios that you miss opportunities for growth, joy, and success.

To break free from the cycle of worry, it's important to shift your focus. Start by identifying the things you can control and take proactive steps to address them. Let go of the rest. Learning to live in the moment, practicing mindfulness, and focusing on solutions rather than problems can significantly reduce your worry. When you channel your energy into productive actions instead of overthinking, you empower yourself to move forward, no matter how uncertain the future may seem.

Worrying about what others think of you, fearing failure, or stressing over every possible outcome only keeps you stuck. You can reclaim your peace by trusting that no matter what happens, you have the strength to handle it.

Taking life one step at a time, without constantly worrying about what lies ahead, will not only improve your mental health but will also make space for personal growth and achievement.

Ask yourself, can you change what you're worrying about? If the answer is yes, then take action. If the answer is no, then worrying serves no purpose. You either have the ability to control the situation or the power to let it go. Worry stems from fear and anxiety, and I've dealt with both for much of my life. The difference now is that I control my fears and anxieties, rather than letting them control me. I wasted so much time and energy worrying about things that never mattered and never came to pass.

Worrying robs us of the present, clouding our vision and distracting us from the precious moments that truly matter. When we learn to manage our emotions instead of being consumed by them, we gain the power to take charge of our lives. By controlling our feelings, we can face challenges with clarity and strength, rather than being held back by unnecessary fear and doubt.

OTHER PEOPLE PERCEPTIONS/OPINIONS ABOUT YOU

What might seem like a perfect life to you may be perceived differently in comparison to someone else. So, the real question boils down to, 'How can we break the cycle of perception?

How can we change how we view ourselves based on the opinions of others?

The feeling of doing everything perfectly can consume your thoughts and mentally drain you for something that rests on someone else's point of view.

What others think of you is not your problem, it is theirs. Most of the time, their opinion of you is entirely wrong. They say things how they see it, not how they are in reality. Honestly, some people feel the need to have an opinion about everything and everyone. It's just how they are. It doesn't have anything to do with you. We ultimately have the choice to let these perceptions control everything we do. The moment we choose to let go of these exterior opinions is the moment we decide to live our lives for ourselves.

TRYING TO PLEASE EVERYONE

If you decide to please everyone, you will suffer as a result. You will say and do things that are going to be against what you believe and think. By trying to please other people, we disrespect ourselves, our struggles, and everything we have worked for. We need to start by finding confidence in ourselves. Tell yourself every day the good things about yourself- the things on the inside that you find to be the most admirable. After you've gone through them all, remind your-self that these are the reasons you trust your own hearts and not the intention of others. It may seem silly or minuscule at first, but continuously enforcing that into your life will give you the motivation to go against the flow.

TAKING EVERYTHING PERSONALLY

If someone has been mean/rude to you, forgive them and don't take it personally. Maybe it didn't have anything to do with you. Perhaps they are having a terrible day, and they wanted to vent to someone. It is not fair, but it happens more than often. People sometimes have bad days. It is not ok, and it should not give everyone a free pass to be rude to others just because they are having a bad day. Although bad behavior isn't always justifiable, by putting yourself in the other person's shoes, you gain insight into why they acted the way they did. This allows you to further empathize with them, which is the first step to moving on.

ANGER

Feeling angry all the time is not suitable for your soul. It just takes away from your happiness and drains your energy. First, you need to acknowledge WHY you are mad or angry. Then, you need to validate your feelings for yourself. Sometimes getting angry is okay. It is a human emotion we all have, and if we didn't get mad sometimes, then no one would stand up for anything- no one would fight for anything. But in the cases where we see it get the best of us, we need to take a look at our situation and assess. We need to know it's okay to have these feelings and remind ourselves that it does not control us.

Sometimes we might feel anger toward someone, and we don't know where it is coming from. Once you find out why you can work towards letting go because it just doesn't serve you.

CONTROL

As much as we want to have authority in every situation, we don't have a say in some parts of our life. If we come across the word control, we should not perceive it as being in command of the situation but rather as how we manage the parts of our lives that we have control over in a healthy way to make the uncontrollable easier to deal with. As much as you try, some things are out of your control.

LIVING IN THE PAST

Stop dwelling about what has already happened; it's in the past, leave it in the past. It's okay to think about it because it is a part of your story, but when we let it consume our lives, it can destroy us. I hear this a lot when people keep bringing up their history and the things they did or didn't do. I feel like it is such a waste of time and energy to be talking or dwelling on the past. You cannot turn back time, can you? Instead, invest your time and energy into something useful like the present time.

Benefits of living in the present moment

Living in the present moment brings a range of profound benefits for personal growth and well-being. One of the most notable advantages is a significant reduction in stress. When you focus on the present, mindfulness practices naturally calm the body's stress response, helping you find peace amidst life's chaos. This focus on the here and now also has a positive impact on mental health, alleviating symptoms of anxiety and depression. By encouraging a positive outlook, mindfulness fosters emotional well-being and a healthier mental state.

Relationships also benefit greatly from living in the moment. Being fully present during interactions strengthens connections, improves communication, and cultivates empathy, making relationships deeper and more fulfilling. Additionally, mindfulness sharpens clarity, allowing you to approach situations with a more balanced perspective, reducing impulsive reactions and fostering thoughtful responses.

Creativity flourishes when the mind is clear and focused. Living in the present opens you up to new ideas and enhances problem-solving abilities. This state of mental clarity also contributes to emotional resilience, as staying present during challenging times helps you navigate difficulties with greater strength and composure.

Physical health is another area positively influenced by mindfulness. The practice has been linked to various health benefits, including better sleep, lower blood pressure, and improved pain management, making it a powerful tool for both mental and physical well-being.

THE FUTURE

We are not there yet! Let go of your worry about what's going to happen in the future. It has not happened yet, and it might not happen at all. So don't worry about it. The anxious feeling of what's going to happen and the overthinking of every little thing will go away in time when we decide to focus our thoughts on the present. We waste precious energy and time when we worry and don't focus on the present. We also miss a lot of opportunities because we are overthinking and overanalyzing what's going to happen.

The Need To Always Be Right

You don't always have to make someone else see your point of view.

Having your own opinions should be enough without explanations.

Sometimes you can't force someone to agree with you about everything.

Past Failures

Whether you have experienced a failed relationship, marriage, or business venture, learn from it. Look at it as proper teaching lessons instead. You can choose to see them as failures, or you can see the positive life lessons out of them. Everything happens for a reason. We make our mistakes as a way for us to learn from them.

So, to flourish in our own time and space, we need to let go of the past, exterior criticism and all negative forces. We need to remind ourselves daily that we can create magic and have confidence in doing so. The sooner we learn this, the sooner we can succeed.

Control The Unexpected

Life happens. Often we plan, and nothing turns out the way we wanted or expected. Planning and staying organized is necessary and beneficial to your everyday life. We often think that the more you get done, the better you know where you are going. But sometimes we forget that some things are out of our control and realm of change. We often beat ourselves up about things we can't change instead of focusing on the things we can. This human response is how we deal with the natural responsibility of decision making versus our feeling of invincibility against natural circumstances. Life happens, and we spend so much time and energy on what could have happened that we forget what is happening now. A way to diagnose when this issue is prevalent in your own life is to ask yourself a simple question, "Is this problem something I can change or cannot change?" Take a moment to ponder and realize that if this problem is something you can change, then great. There is nothing to worry about because there is a way to overcome and achieve. If there isn't something you can do about it - then there is no reason to lose composure because it is out of your hands and therefore not worth your stress. Misinterpreting the power we have over the elements that affect our lives and creating anxiety over things we can't control usually become the foundation of our doubt. Ultimately, this can turn into a domino effect, causing deterioration of your success. Instead of over-analyzing uncontrollable predicaments, a healthier alternative is to arrange your options in such a way that any hiccups in the road ahead can be faced head-on with confidence and composure. Yes, this sounds much easier said than done. But in enough time, with enough practice, your confidence in your path will provide you with the determination to push through what life throws at you. I love surprises- for the most part. However, I am a planner and like to have everything in order. Therefore, surprises throw me off and often give me anxiety no matter how beautiful they are.   No matter what type of personality you have or how well organized you are- life happens- and unexpected events throw us off big time.

Examples of unexpected events:

- You meet someone new

- Dealing with unexpected health problems

- Death in the family

- Unique work or career opportunity

- Job promotion

Can you think of a time in your life that something very unexpected happened and disrupted your life?

This doesn't necessarily have to be a negative disturbance. A disturbance can be anything unexpected that happens and does not give us any advance notice. Due to the natural abruptness of life, we need to make room for these abruptions and adjust our plans accordingly.

Sometimes, the effects of an unexpected bump in the road or a life changing event, can contribute to a sense of vulnerability and insecurity about your goal because you had to change your plans in the first place. Like tripping or falling during a race, we feel like continuing the race to our goal may not be worth trying when down- like we can't catch up — knowing that a change in our plans does not affect the outcome of our success. *Your journey may change,* but with enough hard work and determination, *your destination will not*. Plan with confidence in knowing that with enough effort, your goal can be achieved. The key is to continue your journey with the knowledge that your success is inevitable.

CHAPTER 11

Stop Judging Yourself and Start Observing

STOP JUDGING YOURSELF AND START OBSERVING

If you constantly judge yourself—whether it's how you perform tasks or how you interact with others—you are, in essence, holding yourself back. Constant judgment creates a cycle of negativity, reinforcing self-doubt and undermining your confidence. Every time you scrutinize your actions with a critical eye, you fuel feelings of inadequacy. This inner critic, though perhaps well-intentioned, serves as an obstacle to growth.

Instead, what if you simply observed yourself? Observation, unlike judgment, is neutral. It is a stance of curiosity, not condemnation. Begin by observing how you speak, how you approach tasks, and how you treat others. Instead of labeling these behaviors as "good" or "bad," notice them as they are. Observation creates the space for learning and growth because you can then objectively assess areas where you might want to improve. This shift from judgment to observation is liberating—it transforms your mindset from one of limitation to one of possibility.

THE FIXED MINDSET TRAP

A fixed mindset is one of the biggest roadblocks to personal growth. When you hold onto a fixed mindset, you believe your abilities, intelligence, and potential are static. This creates a fragile self-image, vulnerable to the fear of failure and criticism.

With a fixed mindset:

- Every piece of feedback feels like a personal attack. Instead of viewing it as an opportunity to improve, you take it as an indictment of your worth.

- Change seems impossible. You tell yourself, "This is just who I am," and don't allow yourself the room to grow or evolve.

- You stick to your comfort zone because challenges feel threatening. You might even quit the moment things become difficult, rather than seeing obstacles as part of the learning process.

- Other people's achievements make you feel insecure or jealous, as if their success diminishes your own.

These behaviors reinforce a negative loop that keeps you stuck in the same patterns.

On the other hand, a growth mindset is a catalyst for transformation. It is the belief that you can change, adapt, and improve over time. This mindset fosters resilience and courage, enabling you to take risks, learn from failure, and view challenges as stepping stones toward success.

Examples of a growth mindset include:

88

- Embracing the belief that change and growth are always possible. You know that who you are today doesn't define who you will be tomorrow.

- Viewing past failures as valuable learning experiences. Instead of dwelling on mistakes, you analyze them and use the insights to improve.

- Persevering through setbacks. If something doesn't work out the first time, you try again and again until you succeed.

- Welcoming feedback and constructive criticism. You don't take it personally; instead, you see it as useful information that helps you become better.

- Recognizing that there are no limits to what you can achieve. With effort and the right strategy, you can accomplish anything you set your mind to.

- Feeling inspired, not threatened, by other people's success. You understand that their achievements do not take anything away from you and that success is abundant.

- Loving challenges and pushing yourself out of your comfort zone. You thrive when you're learning new things, even if the process is difficult.

This mindset can transform your daily life. By applying it consistently, you create a solid foundation for personal growth, resilience, and self-awareness.

INTEGRATING THIS MINDSET INTO YOUR LIFE

Transitioning from judgment to observation and adopting a growth mindset takes time, but the rewards are immense. When you become more self-aware, you can assess your relationships, decisions, and everyday challenges with greater clarity and confidence. A growth mindset isn't just about big achievements—it's also about finding success in small, everyday victories.

For example, you might set simple, attainable goals such as organizing your day more effectively or completing a task you've been avoiding. Each accomplishment, no matter how minor, builds momentum and reinforces your belief in your ability to succeed. Over time, these small successes snowball into larger ones.

A healthy mindset is one that's adaptable, organized, and goal-oriented. When you stop worrying about external validation and focus on the things that are within your control, like your mindset and actions, you begin to free yourself from the constraints of fear and self-doubt. It's important to recognize that everyone struggles with these feelings at times. You're not alone in the desire to break free from self-criticism and uncertainty.

BUILDING CONFIDENCE AND CULTIVATING DRIVE

Remember why you started! What is the deeper reason behind your desire to change? Reconnecting with your inner drive can be a powerful motivator as you work toward your goals. Keep your eyes on what you want to improve and focus on becoming the best version of yourself, not the version you think others expect.

As you continue down this path, maintain grace and self-compassion. Building confidence isn't a sprint—it's a journey. There will be missteps along the way, but each one is an opportunity to learn. You deserve to walk your path with the confidence and determination that comes from knowing you're capable of achieving anything you set your mind to.

By shifting your perspective from judgment to observation, from limitation to growth, you'll begin to see yourself as you truly are: a capable, adaptable, and resilient individual who is ready to take on whatever life throws your way.

CHAPTER 12

The 3 C's: Confidence, Commitment, Courage

If you want to succeed at anything, commitment will be your strongest ally, while procrastination will be your greatest enemy. Commitment pushes you forward, while procrastination holds you back, creating excuses and delays. You must hold yourself accountable for everything you do or don't do. Success doesn't come from waiting for the perfect moment or having all the skills upfront—it comes from showing up and staying dedicated. Even if you lack the necessary skills, with enough commitment and persistence, you can still achieve your goals.

It's crucial to understand that being busy and being productive are not the same thing. Too often, we equate a full schedule with progress, but that's not always the case. When I ask someone, "How are you doing?" the common response is, "Good, just working – very busy." My answer used to be the same, no matter what phase of life I was in.

Whether I was:

- Staying at home with one child,

- Working while raising two children,

- Attending college with two kids,

- Pregnant while working full-time and going to college,

- Raising four kids and attending college,

- Or working full-time while managing a household of four children

I was always busy. And now, even when I work from home with four kids, the answer is the same: Busy! But are we truly productive?That's the real question. We all have packed schedules, but how effectively are we managing our time?

Being busy often gives us the illusion of productivity, but real progress comes from intentional action, not just movement. We can fill our days with tasks and still be far from reaching our goals. So, it's essential to step back and evaluate: How are we managing our time? Are we prioritizing what truly matters, or just filling our hours with tasks that keep us in motion without moving us forward?

This is where commitment comes into play. You may feel like you don't have time to achieve your goals because you are too busy. However, when you commit to doing whatever it takes, you begin to prioritize your goals and improve your time management skills. Commitment is about more than just showing up—it's about focusing on the right things, making the most of your time, and staying dedicated even when it's hard. When you learn to manage your time and energy well, you shift from just being busy to being productive, making real strides toward success.

Once your priorities are in order, you'll make time for what truly matters.

For five years, I spent most of my weekends studying, doing homework, and preparing for exams instead of spending time with my family because I was committed to graduating. My goal was so important that I made sacrifices, but I made sure to spend quality time with my family during semester breaks. Without that level of commitment, I might have quit or failed multiple times. I held myself accountable, and I refused to make excuses.

In the realm of personal growth, few principles are as crucial as effective time management. It serves as a guiding star, helping us maximize productivity, develop strategies for managing time efficiently, and sharpen our skills in prioritization and decision-making. This chapter delves into the profound importance of managing time wisely, offering insights into how to make the most of each moment while aligning your actions with your goals.

MAXIMIZING PRODUCTIVITY

Time is one of our most finite and valuable resources, and how we manage it has a direct impact on our personal growth. Maximizing productivity involves optimizing how we use our time and energy to achieve our goals. The key to this lies in developing a structured approach that not only allows for the completion of tasks but also creates space for meaningful growth and self-care.

Efficiency is one of the main benefits of effective time management. When you thoughtfully organize your day and tasks, you can achieve more in less time. This results in reduced stress since a well-organized schedule brings order and eliminates the chaos that can arise from poor planning. Time management also brings you closer to your goals by ensuring that you dedicate time to the activities that matter most to you, whether that's in your career, personal development, or relationships.

Balancing work and personal life is another significant outcome of managing your time well. By streamlining your schedule, you can make room for hobbies, rest, and relationships that bring fulfillment. Effective time management also supports continuous learning, providing regular opportunities for self-improvement. With each accomplishment, you build confidence and affirm your abilities, further propelling your personal growth journey.

STRATEGIES FOR EFFECTIVE TIME MANAGEMENT

To maximize productivity and fully harness the power of time management, it's essential to establish clear strategies that support your goals. Setting clear goals is a crucial first step. When you define your short-term and long-term aspirations, you give yourself a sense of purpose, which helps guide your daily actions. Prioritizing tasks is also vital, as not all activities carry the same weight. Techniques like time-blocking can help you allocate specific chunks of time to important tasks, minimizing distractions and keeping you on track.

Maintaining a planner or calendar ensures that deadlines and responsibilities are met, while eliminating time-wasting activities like excessive screen time or procrastination frees up valuable hours. Another key tactic is delegating tasks when possible. Learning when to ask for help or assign responsibilities can create more time for critical endeavors. Focusing on one task at a time, also known as single-tasking, is far more efficient than trying to juggle multiple things at once.

Setting self-imposed deadlines can enhance motivation and create a sense of urgency that keeps you moving forward. Utilizing time management tools and apps can further assist in organizing your day, tracking progress, and keeping tasks in order. Lastly, regular breaks are important for sustaining productivity over the long haul. Short moments of rest allow your mind to recharge, improving focus and effectiveness.

PRIORITIZATION AND DECISION-MAKING

Managing your time wisely requires more than just organizing tasks; it demands the ability to make informed decisions about how to spend your time and where to focus your energy. Prioritization is an art that involves evaluating tasks and commitments to determine their importance and aligning them with your broader goals.

To sharpen your prioritization skills, it's important to clarify your top priorities in both the short term and long term. Reflect on what matters most to you, and align your daily activities with those values. Evaluating the potential impact of each task is also key—will it significantly contribute to your goals, or is it less important in the grand scheme of things?

Urgency can sometimes cloud our judgment, so it's essential to distinguish between tasks that are truly urgent and those that are not. Aligning your efforts with your long-term objectives helps to maintain focus and motivation. At times, this might mean learning to say no to commitments that don't align with your priorities or that stretch your capacity too thin.

It's also valuable to consider both the time and energy required for each task. Some tasks may take longer but are less mentally demanding, while others require intense focus but might be quicker to complete. Periodic reflection on your priorities is essential, as they may shift over time. Maintaining a decision journal can help you track important decisions and their outcomes, providing insight for future choices.

Time management is a cornerstone of personal growth. By maximizing productivity, implementing efficient strategies, and refining your decision-making and prioritization skills, you gain control over your time and, ultimately, the trajectory of your life. Effective time management allows you to align your daily actions with your long-term goals, bringing you closer to achieving the life you envision.

Making excuses or blaming life's obstacles will only pull you further away from your goals.

It allows you to justify your lack of motivation and delay your dreams. Instead, follow these steps to stay on track:

1. Find an accountability partner: Choose someone who understands your journey and can motivate you when you feel stuck or unmotivated.

2. Commit to your schedule and your goals: Be careful not to overcommit. Avoid taking on tasks that aren't aligned with your priorities just to stay busy or to avoid addressing more critical situations.

Once you prioritize your life and commit to your goals, confidence, commitment, and courage will guide you:

1. Confidence: Believe in yourself and build inner strength.

2. Commitment: Dedicate yourself fully to your goals, no matter what it takes.

3. Courage: Develop the bravery to take risks and forge your own path.

By believing in yourself, you increase your chances of success. Knowing that you are capable of achieving anything gives you the courage to stay committed to your goals. Embracing your truth gives you a reason to stay devoted to your dreams.

A prime example of how determination can drive commitment is my personal journey through college. I had the confidence to believe in myself, the commitment to keep going, and the courage to start. I had no mentors and no one to encourage me. I had to convince myself to take one step at a time. It was important to me, and I had many "whys" to keep me going.

Initially, I lacked the confidence to even apply for college. Questions like "What if I fail?" and "What if I don't understand the lectures", "What if my kids get sick, and I have to miss class?" kept me from moving forward. My doubts held me back, but once I found the courage to take that first step, I broke free from my own overthinking.

Courage isn't about being fearless; it's about acknowledging your fears and moving forward despite them. When you gather the courage to leave your comfort zone, you gain the confidence you need to focus on your goals. Courage reveals who you truly are.

The comfort zone doesn't necessarily mean a place of happiness—it just means it's the life you know. Anything outside of that can feel terrifying, but pushing past those fears leads to growth. Whether it's leaving a job, speaking up, or asking for help, courage is essential. Sometimes, we believe courage means acting without fear, but real courage comes from recognizing fear and refusing to let it stop us. When we do that, we gain the confidence we need to focus on our goals. Courage shows us the path to becoming our true selves.

CONCLUSION

The journey of personal growth is a remarkable odyssey, a quest that takes us from who we are to who we aspire to be. It is a journey marked by transformation, self-discovery, and the continuous pursuit of self-improvement. As we conclude this exploration of the "Empowering You-12 Key Principles for Personal Growth," let us reflect on the profound significance of this expedition.

The quest for personal growth is not a linear path but a dynamic process, a kaleidoscope of experiences, challenges, and triumphs. It's a journey marked by constant evolution, an ongoing commitment to becoming the best version of ourselves. Along this path, we've explored the foundational principles that underpin personal growth, each revealing its unique facets and wisdom.

From the importance of self-awareness to the significance of adaptability, we've delved into the core principles that empower us to thrive in a complex and ever-changing world. We've celebrated the power of positive thinking and mindfulness, learning to navigate time and resources effectively, and the vital importance of emotional intelligence and self-care. We've embraced the transformative potential of gratitude and giving back, infusing our lives with meaning and connection.

This journey is a testament to the human spirit's capacity for growth, resilience, and evolution. It's a reminder that personal growth is not a destination but a lifelong commitment. Each principle and step we take moves us closer to reaching our full potential, discovering our true selves, and making a positive impact on our communities and the world.

The journey of personal growth is a reflection of the human condition, a journey that transcends boundaries, cultures, and time. It's a shared endeavor that unites us in our collective aspiration to lead fulfilling lives, find purpose, and make a positive impact. It reminds us that we are all fellow travelers on this path, learning, growing, and evolving together.

As we conclude this exploration, let us recognize that personal growth is not a solitary endeavor but a collective one. We learn from each other, inspire one another, and uplift those around us. In our pursuit of self-improvement, we also contribute to the growth of the world, making it a better place for all.

So, let us celebrate this journey, embrace the principles that guide us, and continue to evolve, knowing that the quest for personal growth is a lifelong adventure filled with limitless opportunities and the promise of a brighter, more fulfilling future. In the spirit of personal growth, let us keep moving forward, ever upward, and ever closer to the best versions of ourselves.

BONUS

Here is a list of simple things we can do now to improve and enhance our life.

1. Read more books- Plan for reading 20 min every day 2. Start your day with gratitude- Write down every day three things you are grateful for

3. Donating

4. Volunteering

5. Meditation

6. Take time off from electronics-social media-phone

7. Clean out social media- Organize your feed and what/who you follow. Follow only the accounts that feed positivity and creativity.

8. Organize your home-closet-garage-basement

9. Get a good night's sleep

10. Create a daily routine

11. Exercise for 20 min- take a walk outdoors

12. Be present

13. Find something you enjoy doing in your free time

14. Plan ahead

15. Get a planner and organize your schedule

16. Try something new food- new exercise- a new place to visit

17. Go somewhere you have never been before if possible

18. Get rid of debt

19. Give back- charity- donation- church

20. Find time to rewind

21. Eat healthy

22. Make small steps each day for a healthier lifestyle

23. Be kind to yourself

24. Give up bad habits

25. Smile more

26. Get rid of toxic people in your life

27. Focus on your goals

28. Make a vision board for your goals

29. Look at your vision board every day

30. Find a hobby that makes you happy

31. Spend time with friends and family

32. Don't be afraid to ask for help

33. Listen to your favorite music

34. Watch your favorite movie

35. Learn something new

36. Listen to any personal growth podcast - My top choices are "On Purpose" with Jay Shetty and "Mindvalley Show" with Vishen

37. Laugh more

38. Practice daily gratitude

39. Pray more

40. Take control of your finances

41. Don't procrastinate

42. Plan in advance

43. Block your time

44. Get out of your comfort zone more often

100 DAILY AFFIRMATIONS TO CREATE A POSITIVE MINDSET

1. I am capable of achieving anything I set my mind to.

2. I embrace challenges as opportunities for growth.

3. I am deserving of success and happiness.

4. I am confident in my abilities.

5. I attract positive experiences into my life.

6. I focus on the present moment and let go of the past.

7. I am surrounded by love and support.

8. I am resilient and can overcome any obstacle.

9. I am worthy of love and respect.

10. I believe in my dreams and have the courage to pursue them.

11. I am grateful for all the blessings in my life.

12. I radiate positivity and attract positive people.

13. I am constantly evolving and becoming a better version of myself.

14. I have the power to create my own happiness.

15. I trust myself to make the right decisions.

16. I release all negative thoughts and embrace positivity.

17. I am open to new opportunities and possibilities.

18. I forgive myself for past mistakes and move forward with a clean slate.

19. I am in control of my own happiness.

20. I am worthy of love and affection.

21. I am capable of achieving my goals with focus and determination.

22. I am surrounded by abundance and prosperity.

23. I attract positive relationships into my life.

24. I choose to see the beauty in every situation.

25. I am proud of my accomplishments, no matter how big or small.

26. I trust in life and know that everything happens for a reason.

27. I have the power to change my thoughts and create a positive mindset.

28. I embrace uncertainty and see it as an opportunity for growth.

29. I am worthy of success and all the good things life offers.

30. I am in control of my own destiny.

31. I choose to focus on solutions rather than problems.

32. I am deserving of love and happiness.

33. I am grateful for my body and treat it with love and respect.

34. I have the ability to overcome any challenge that

comes my way.

35. I attract abundance in all areas of my life.

36. Positive and supportive people surround me.

37. I am a magnet for success and prosperity.

38. I trust in my intuition and make decisions with confidence.

39. I am worthy of all the love and joy in the world.

40. I am grateful for the lessons I have learned and the growth I have experienced.

41. I am courageous and can face any fear that arises. 42. I am patient and trust that everything will unfold in perfect timing.

43. I choose to let go of negativity and embrace positivity.

44. I am grateful for the opportunities that come my way.

45. I am proud of myself for the progress I have made.

46. I am open to receiving all the good things the universe offers.

47. I am filled with energy and vitality.

48. I am deserving of abundance and success in all areas of my life.

49. I am resilient and bounce back from setbacks with strength.

50. I am confident in expressing my true self.

51. I attract positive and fulfilling relationships into my life.

52. I release all self-doubt and believe in my own abilities.

53. I am grateful for the support and love I receive from others.

54. I am a magnet for opportunities that align with my passions and purpose.

55. I am surrounded by beauty and find joy in the simple things.

56. I trust that the universe is always working in my favor.

57. I am capable of achieving greatness.

58. I release all negative attachments from the past and embrace the present moment.

59. I am worthy of abundance and success in all areas of my life.

60. I have the power to create a positive and fulfilling life. 61. I am resilient and can overcome any challenge that comes my way.

62. I am grateful for the lessons I have learned and the growth I have experienced.

63. I am confident in my abilities and trust in my own judgment.

64. I attract positive and supportive people into my life.

65. I am open to receiving all the blessings and opportunities that come my way.

66. I release all self-doubt and embrace my inner strength.

67. I am worthy of love, happiness, and success.

68. I trust in life and know that everything happens for a reason.

69. I am proud of myself for my progress and the person I am becoming.

70. I am deserving of all the good things that life has to offer.

71. I am grateful for the abundance and prosperity that surrounds me.

72. I radiate positivity and attract positive experiences into my life.

73. I am capable of achieving my goals and dreams.

74. I trust in my intuition and make decisions with confidence.

75. I choose to see the good in every situation and find joy in the present moment.

76. I am deserving of love, respect, and kindness.

77. I release all negative thoughts and replace them with positive affirmations.

78. I am open to receiving love, joy, and abundance in all areas of my life.

79. I am grateful for the opportunities that come my way and embrace them enthusiastically.

80. I am resilient and bounce back from challenges with grace and determination.

81. I am confident in my abilities and trust in my own judgment.

82. I attract positive and like-minded people into my life.

83. I am worthy of success and all the good things life offers. 84. I trust in the divine plan and know that everything is unfolding perfectly.

85. I am proud of myself for my progress and the person I am becoming.

86. I am grateful for the abundance and prosperity that flows into my life.

87. I radiate positivity and attract positive experiences.

88. I am capable of achieving my goals and dreams.

89. I trust in my intuition and make decisions with confidence.

90. I focus on the present moment and let go of past regrets.

91. I am deserving of love, happiness, and success. 92. I release all self-doubt and embrace my inner strength.

93. I am open to receiving all the blessings that come my way.

94. I am grateful for the lessons I have learned and the growth I have experienced.

95. I am confident in my abilities and trust in my own judgment.

96. I attract positive and supportive relationships into my life.

97. I am worthy of love, joy, and abundance.

98. I trust in the process of life and know that everything is unfolding perfectly.

99. I am proud of myself for my progress and the person I am becoming.

100. I am grateful for all the blessings and opportunities that came my way.

MY FAVORITE QUOTES ABOUT PERSONAL GROWTH

"It is never too late for a new beginning in your life."
- Joyce Meyers

"Continued improvement is better than delayed perfection."
- Mark Twain

"It seems impossible until it's done."
- Nelson Mandela

"Change is painful, but nothing is as painful as being stuck somewhere you don't belong."
- N.R Narayana Murthy

"The 3 C's of life: change, chances, choices."
- Zig Ziglar

"Difficult roads often lead to beautiful destinations."
- Zig Ziglar

"Work hard in silence ... let your success be the noise."
- Frank Ocean

"The best way to predict your future is to create it."
- Abraham Lincoln

"I am building from every mistake I have made." - Mandy Hale

"Fear is a reaction ... courage is a decision."
- Sir Winston Churchill

"Do what you have to do until you can do what you want to do."
- Oprah Winfrey

"The best investment is an investment in yourself."

- Warren Buffet

ABOUT THE AUTHOR

Anisa Marku is a prolific author, known for SMART Goals Mastery and 12 Principles for Personal Growth. As an Albanian immigrant who moved from Germany to Michigan, Anisa has faced many challenges, including dropping out of high school at 16 years old. However, through determination and goal-setting, she transformed her life. Now a successful entrepreneur and mother of four, she uses her platform to inspire others to set goals and embrace personal growth. Her journey exemplifies resilience, the power of education, and the pursuit of one's passions.

Connect with Anisa:

Email: anisa05@me.com

IG: anisa05

FB: Anisa Marku

ACKNOWLEDGMENTS

Many thanks to everyone who has supported, helped and contributed to this book's production. I am forever grateful for this opportunity which may have been possible without your help.

Can You Help?

Thank You So Much For Taking Your Time and Reading My Book!

I appreciate all of your feedback, and I love hearing what you have to say.

I need your input to improve this book's next version and future books.

Please leave me an honest review on Amazon, letting me know what you think of the book.

Thanks so much!

Anisa Marku

www.ingramcontent.com/pod-product-compliance
Lightning Source LLC
Chambersburg PA
CBHW061658120626
46550CB00003B/991